David Mamet
Plays: 4

Oleanna, The Cryptogram
The Old Neighborhood

'DAVID MAMET has a miraculous ear for the heightened music of American dialect – it makes poetry out of common usage' *New York Post*

Oleanna: 'An exploration of male-female conflicts [which] cogently demonstrates that when free thought and dialogue are imperilled, nobody wins' *Independent*

The Cryptogram: 'Here is the finest American playwright of his generation at full stretch. The writing is tight, spare, and as accurate and ruthless as a scalpel' *Sunday Times*

The Old Neighborhood: 'Mamet, ranked with Miller, Albee and Shepard as America's finest living playwrights, distills the raw, rank flavour of people wading down streams of consciousness . . . A play of riveting disquiet' *Evening Standard*

David Mamet was born in Chicago in 1947. He studied at Goddard College, Vermont (where he was later Artist-in-Residence), and at the Neighborhood Playhouse School of Theater in New York. His first and many subsequent plays were first performed by the St Nicholas Theater Company, Chicago, of which he was a founding member and Artistic Director. He is the author of the plays *Oleanna*; *Glengarry Glenn Ross*, for which he won a Pulitzer Prize and a New York Drama Critics Circle Award; *Speed the Plow*; and *Sexual Perversity in Chicago*, among others. His films include, as screenwriter, *The Postman Always Rings Twice*, *The Verdict*, *The Untouchables*, *The Edge* and *Wag the Dog*, and as a writer/director, *House of Games*, *Homicide*, *Things Change*, *The Spanish Prisoner* and *State and Main*. He is also the author of children's books, four books of essays, two novels and a book on acting, *True and False*.

by the same author and also available from Methuen

Mamet Plays: One
(Duck Variations, Sexual Perversity in Chicago, Squirrels, American
Buffalo, The Water Engine, Mr Happiness)

Mamet Plays: Two
(Reunion, Dark Pony, A Life in the Theatre, The Woods,
Lakeboat, Edmond)

Mamet Plays: Three
(Glengarry Glen Ross, Prairie du Chien, The Shawl, Speed-the-Plow)

American Buffalo
Boston Marriage
The Cryptogram
Glengarry Glen Ross
The Old Neighborhood
Oleanna
Speed-the-Plow
State and Main

DAVID MAMET

Plays: 4

Oleanna
The Cryptogram
The Old Neighborhood

Introduced by the author

Methuen Drama

METHUEN CONTEMPORARY DRAMATISTS

1 3 5 7 9 10 8 6 4 2

This collection first published in Great Britain in 2002
by Methuen Publishing Limited
215 Vauxhall Bridge Road, London SW1V 1EJ

Oleanna was first published by Methuen in 1993
Copyright © 1993 by David Mamet

The Cryptogram was first published by Methuen in 1995
Copyright © 1995 by David Mamet

The Old Neighborhood was first published by Methuen in 1998
Copyright © 1998 by David Mamet

Collection copyright © 2002 David Mamet
Introduction copyright © 2002 David Mamet

The author has asserted his moral rights.

Methuen Publishing Limited Reg. No. 3543167

A CIP catalogue record for this book
is available from the British Library

ISBN 0 413 77132 6

Typeset by Deltatype Ltd, Birkenhead, Merseyside
Printed and bound in Great Britain by
Cox & Wyman Ltd, Reading, Berkshire

Contents

David Mamet:
A Chronology

PLAYS	USA	UK
Duck Variations, St Nicholas Theater Company, Chicago, 1972; Regent Theatre, London, 1977	1972	1977
Sexual Perversity in Chicago, Organic Theater Co., Chicago, 1974; Regent Theatre, London, 1977	1974	1977
Squirrels, St Nicholas Theater Company, Chicago, 1974; King's Head Theatre, London, 1993	1974	1993
American Buffalo, Goodman Theater Company, Chicago, 1975; National Theatre, London, 1978	1975	1978
Reunion, St Nicholas Theater Company, Chicago, 1976	1976	
The Woods, St Nicholas Theater Company, Chicago, 1977	1977	
The Water Engine, St Nicholas Theater Company, Chicago, 1977; Hampstead Theatre, London, 1989	1977	1989
A Life in the Theatre, Goodman Theater, Chicago; Theatre de Lys, New York, 1977; Brighton, 1989	1977	1989
Mr Happiness, New York Shakespeare Festival, New York, 1978	1978	
Prairie du Chien, National Public Radio, 1979; Royal Court Theatre Upstairs, London, 1986	1979	1986
Lakeboat, Court Street Theater, Milwaukee Rep, Milwaukee, WI, 1980	1980	

SCREENPLAYS

Introduction

Recognition, Reversal and Aesthetic Distance

Here we have two classical tragedies and a hermaphrodite drama. *Oleanna* has a protagonist, a deuteragonist and a telephone. The telephone functions, as per usual, as a chorus or title card – to introduce new information, emotional or factual, or to comment upon the old.

The Cryptogram is unusual, formally, in this: the identities of the pro- and deuteragonist are not revealed until the climax of the play, and it is, therefore, the *audience* which experiences recognition and, so, sees the reversal of the situation of the characters. It is revealed that Del, and not the child, is the clown, or chorus, and that the child is the protagonist and the story is his.

I seem to have written four classical tragedies, the two named above, *American Buffalo* and *The Woods*. These are classical in their adherence to the Aristotelian unities, the strictures of time, place and action. They show the High (the Hero) brought low, and, at the play's conclusion, couple reversal of the situation and recognition on the part of the Hero.

These plays – though I wouldn't have mentioned it at the time of their first productions (producers are notably skittish and the Press are very much what we know them to be) – are all written in free verse.

FEAR AND PITY, CATHARSIS, ETC . . .

We recognise ourselves in the characters of tragedy, and, so, experience fear. We can imagine ourselves in their situation. And, as there is a distance between us and them – the much mentioned 'aesthetic distance' – we are allowed to feel pity for them – that is, we know that they are *not* ourselves. (In the historical drama, in the *roman à clef*, or the tell-all dramatisation the aesthetic distance has been removed. We may feel salacious interest, but can neither fear nor pity. The phrase 'Based on a true story', similarly, can only vitiate any power the drama [*qua* drama] may have possessed.)

In the hubristic, blind, or otherwise self-absorbed gropings of the hero towards his goal (that is to say, his destruction), we see our own human state: supposedly free to act, but each elaboration of freedom-of-choice bringing us closer to the realisation that we are bound. We are bound by our character, by our lack of self-knowledge, by the inscrutable ways of gods. To recognise this, and to avow it, is to lay our burden down, to surrender – which is the meaning of *catharsis*. Or, as Shakespeare had it: 'When remedy is exhausted, so is Grief'.

GUILT

Shakespeare has Hamlet tell Horatio that he has heard that guilty creatures, sitting at a play, may so forget themselves as to enter into spontaneous self-confession. I always thought it poetic hyperbole, but I found that it is, in fact, possible. I saw such transport operate, night after night, during the first New York run of my play *Oleanna*.

I saw audience members scream at the actors, fight with each other after and even during the play; I saw couples dispute their opposed interpretations of the piece, vociferously and even physically, long after the final curtain. I saw audience members berate, and, in one case, even strike a home-bound actor.

The play moved the audience out of itself.

The cant of the times, the rabid demand for hypocrisy, and its attendant burden of fear, was loosed by the play. The aesthetic distance allowed the audience to suspend its reasoning power (and that power's attendant capacity for hypocrisy), and the (variously interpretable) viciousness, blindness, condescension and savagery of the characters in the play moved the audience to fear and, regularly, to rage. Quite a compliment.

In *The Cryptogram* they felt pity for the boy's state and were moved that the nature of his sufferings was not fully revealed till the close of the play, and the revelation that the play was about him (that is, about *them*).

It is, of course, easy to feel pity for a child – they are like us, and *not* like us. We may pity them while maintaining an aesthetic distance, or, in a phrase disgraced by politicians, *deniability*.

DRAMA

The Old Neighborhood falls out of the genre of tragedy and straight into that of drama; precisely, into that sub-genre which used to be known as 'kitchen-sink' (e.g. *Look Back in Anger, Hatful of Rain, A View from the Bridge*).

The play is, of course, just three one-act plays with the same protagonist – three visions of 'the trip home'. Both the subject and the form are modern, grown out, let me pontificate, of the late Industrial Revolution and the decampment from the Land. The form was first popularised, indeed, invented by Chekhov, in his great quartet, *The Cherry Orchard*, etc . . . , notably plotless, character pieces treating the outsider(s) against the homefolk. These plays are, in fact, sketches which replace the plot (most active in tragedy) with a prolonged comment or conceit about the nature of stasis. (*Vide: The Waters of the Moon, Truckline Café, The Lower Depths* and *Virginia Woolf*, this last a vastly better play, and approaching tragedy.)

Stanislavski wrote that tragedy stands in the same relation to melodrama that drama does to comedy.

I find the insight useful, as this drama (*The Old Neighborhood*), and those mentioned *supra*, can, by squinting, be seen as comedies. (Chekhov, in fact, referred to his plays as such.) They rely upon manufacturing incidents to reveal character, which incidents might as well be gags; and, at the play's end, the protagonist is surprised to find him or herself right back where they started.

As the reader may have judged, considerations of form fascinate me.

Jack Aubrey, we are told, sailed the seas by rule-of-thumb, until, late in his life, he fell in love with spherical trigonometry.

Similarly, the more plays and films I wrote, the more I saw that attention to structural considerations constituted both wisdom and good financial planning, as such attention tended to put food on the table.

A prestigious writers' group informed me latterly (August

2001) that I had been selected to receive their Lifetime
Achievement Award. I expressed my gratitude and told
them, Thanks, but I'm not done yet. I hope it's true.

David Mamet
Chicago, 2001

Oleanna

This play is dedicated to the memory of
Michael Merrit

Oleanna was first performed in the United States, at the American Repertory Theatre Massachusetts, on 1 May 1992.

Oleanna was first performed in the United Kingdom at the Royal Court Theatre, London, on 24 June 1993. The cast was as follows:

John   David Suchet
Carol   Lia Williams

Directed by Harold Pinter
Designed by Eileen Diss
Lighting by Gerry Jenkinson
Sound by Lorna Earl

Act One

John *is talking on the phone.* **Carol** *is seated across the desk from him.*

John (*on phone*)   And what about the land. (*Pause.*) The land. And what about the land? (*Pause.*) What about it? (*Pause.*) No. I don't understand. Well, yes, I'm I'm ... no, I'm *sure* it's signif ... I'm sure it's significant. (*Pause.*) Because it's significant to mmmmmm ... did you call Jerry? (*Pause.*) Because ... no, no, no, no, no. What did they say ... ? Did you speak to the *real* estate ... where *is* she ... ? Well, well, all right. Where are her notes? Where are the notes we took with her. (*Pause.*) I thought you were? No. No, I'm sorry, I didn't mean that, I just thought that I saw you, when we were there ... what ... ? I thought I saw you with a *pencil*. WHY NOW? is what I'm say ... well, that's why I say 'call Jerry.' Well, I can't right now, be ... no, I *didn't* schedule any ... Grace: I *didn't* ... I'm well aware ... Look: Look. Did you call Jerry? Will you call Jerry ... ? Because I can't now. I'll be there, I'm sure I'll be there in fifteen, in twenty. I intend to. No, we aren't *going* to lose the, we aren't *going* to lose the house. Look: Look, I'm not minimizing it. The 'easement.' Did she say 'easement'? (*Pause.*) What did she *say; is* it a 'term of art,' are we *bound* by it ... I'm sorry ... (*Pause.*) are: we: yes. *Bound* by ... Look: (*He checks his watch.*) before the other side *goes home*, all right? 'a term of art.' Because: that's right (*Pause.*) The yard for the boy. Well, that's the whole ... Look: I'm going to meet you there ... (*He checks his watch.*) Is the realtor there? All right, tell her to show you the basement again. Look at the *this* because ... Bec ... I'm leaving in, I'm leaving in ten or fifteen ... Yes. No, no, I'll meet you at the new ... That's a good. If he thinks it's necc ... you tell Jerry to meet ... All right? We *aren't* going to lose the deposit. All right? I'm sure it's going to be ... (*Pause.*) I hope so. (*Pause.*) I love you, too. (*Pause.*) I love you, too. As soon as ... I will.

(*He hangs up.*) (*He bends over the desk and makes a note.*) (*He looks up.*) (*To* **Carol**.) I'm sorry . . .

Carol (*pause*)   What is a 'term of art'?

John (*pause*)   I'm sorry . . . ?

Carol (*pause*)   What is a 'term of art'?

John   Is that what you want to talk about?

Carol   . . . to talk about . . . ?

John   Let's take the mysticism out of it, shall we? Carol? (*Pause.*) Don't you think? I'll tell you: when you have some 'thing.' Which must be broached. (*Pause.*) Don't you think . . . ? (*Pause.*)

Carol   . . . don't I think . . . ?

John   Mmm?

Carol   . . . did I . . . ?

John   . . . what?

Carol   Did . . . did I . . . did I say something wr . . .

John (*pause*)   No. I'm sorry. No. You're right. I'm very sorry. I'm somewhat rushed. As you see. I'm sorry. You're right. (*Pause.*) What is a 'term of art'? It seems to mean a *term*, which has come, through its use, to mean something *more specific* than the words would, to someone *not acquainted* with them . . . indicate. That, I believe, is what a 'term of art,' would mean. (*Pause.*)

Carol   You don't know what it means . . . ?

John   I'm not sure that I know what it means. It's one of those things, perhaps you've had them, that, you look them up, or have someone explain them to you, and you say 'aha,' and, you immediately *forget* what . . .

Carol   You don't do that.

John   . . . I . . . ?

Carol   You don't do . . .

John ... I don't, what ...?

Carol ... for ...

John ... I don't for ...

Carol ... no ...

John ... forget things? Everybody does that.

Carol No, they don't.

John They don't ...

Carol No.

John (*pause*) No. Everybody does that.

Carol Why would they do that ...?

John Because. I don't know. Because it doesn't interest them.

Carol No.

John I think so, though. (*Pause.*) I'm sorry that I was distracted.

Carol You don't have to say that to me.

John You paid me the compliment, or the 'obeisance' – all right – of coming in here ... All right. *Carol*. I find that I am at a *standstill*. I find that I ...

Carol ... what ...

John ... one moment. In regard to your ... to your ...

Carol Oh, oh. You're buying a new house!

John No, let's get on with it.

Carol 'get on'? (*Pause*).

John I know how ... *believe* me. I know how ... potentially *humiliating* these ... I have no desire to ... I have no desire other than to help you. But: (*He picks up some papers on his desk.*) I won't even say 'but.' I'll say that as I go back over the ...

Carol I'm just, I'm just trying to . . .

John . . . no, it will not do.

Carol . . . what? What will . . . ?

John No. I see, I see what you, it . . . (*He gestures to the papers.*) but your work . . .

Carol I'm just: I sit in class I . . . (*She holds up her notebook.*) I take notes . . .

John (*simultaneously with 'notes'*) Yes. I understand. What I am trying to *tell* you is that some, some basic . . .

Carol . . . I . . .

John . . . one moment: some basic missed communi . . .

Carol I'm doing what I'm told. I bought your book, I read your . . .

John No. I'm sure you . . .

Carol No, no, no. I'm doing what I'm told. It's *difficult* for me. It's *difficult* . . .

John . . . but . . .

Carol I don't . . . lots of the *language* . . .

John . . . please . . .

Carol The *language*, the 'things' that you say . . .

John I'm sorry. No. I don't think that that's true.

Carol It *is* true. I . . .

John I think . . .

Carol It *is* true.

John . . . I . . .

Carol Why would I . . . ?

John I'll tell you why: you're an incredibly bright girl.

Carol . . . I . . .

John   You're an incredibly . . . you have no problem with the . . . Who's kidding who?

Carol   . . . I . . .

John   No. No. I'll tell you why. I'll tell . . . I think you're *angry*, I . . .

Carol   . . . why would I . . .

John   . . . wait one moment. I . . .

Carol   It *is* true. I have *problems* . . .

John   . . . every . . .

Carol   . . . I come from a different *social* . . .

John   . . . ev . . .

Carol   a different economic . . .

John   . . . Look:

Carol   No. I: when I *came* to this school:

John   Yes. Quite . . . (*Pause.*)

Carol   . . . does that mean nothing . . . ?

John   . . . but look: look . . .

Carol   . . . I . . .

John   (*picks up paper*)   Here: Please: Sit down. (*Pause.*) Sit down. (*Reads from her paper.*) 'I think that the ideas contained in this work express the author's feelings in a way that he intended, based on his results.' What can that mean? Do you see? What . . .

Carol   I, the best that I . . .

John   I'm saying, that perhaps this course . . .

Carol   No, no, no, you can't, you can't . . . I have to . . .

John   . . . how . . .

Carol   . . . I have to pass it . . .

John Carol, I:

Carol I *have* to pass this course, I . . .

John Well.

Carol . . . don't you . . .

John Either the . . .

Carol . . . I . . .

John . . . either the, I . . . either the *criteria* for judging progress in the class are . . .

Carol No, no, no, no, I have to pass it.

John Now, look: I'm a human being, I . . .

Carol I did what you told me. I did, I did everything that, I read your *book*, you told me to buy your book and read it. Everything you *say* I . . . (*She gestures to her notebook.*) (*The phone rings.*) I do. . . . Ev . . .

John . . . look:

Carol . . . everything I'm told . . .

John Look. Look. I'm not your *father*. (*Pause.*)

Carol What?

John I'm.

Carol Did I say you were my father?

John . . . no . . .

Carol Why did you say that . . . ?

John I . . .

Carol . . . why . . . ?

John . . . in class I . . . (*He picks up the phone.*) (*Into phone:*) Hello. I can't talk now. Jerry? Yes? I underst . . . I can't talk now. I know . . . I know . . . Jerry. I can't *talk* now. Yes, I. Call me back in . . . Thank you. (*He hangs up.*) (*To* **Carol**.) What do you want me to do? We are two people, all right? Both of whom have subscribed to . . .

Carol No, no . . .

John . . . certain arbitrary . . .

Carol No. You have to help me.

John Certain institutional . . . you tell me what you want me to do. . . . You tell me what you want me to . . .

Carol How can I go back and tell them the *grades* that I . . .

John . . . what can I do . . . ?

Carol *Teach* me. *Teach* me.

John . . . I'm trying to teach you.

Carol I read your book. I read it. I don't under . . .

John . . . you don't understand it.

Carol No.

John Well, perhaps it's not well *written* . . .

Carol (*simultaneously with 'written'*) No. No. No. I want to *understand* it.

John What don't you understand? (*Pause.*)

Carol *Any* of it. What you're trying to say. When you talk about . . .

John . . . yes . . . ? (*She consults her notes.*)

Carol 'Virtual warehousing of the young' . . .

John 'Virtual warehousing of the young.' If we artificially prolong adolescence . . .

Carol . . . and about 'The Curse of Modern Education.'

John . . . well . . .

Carol I don't . . .

John Look. It's just a *course*, it's just a *book*, it's just a . . .

Carol   No. No. There are *people* out there. People who came *here*. To know something they didn't *know*. Who *came* here. To be *helped*. To be *helped*. So someone would *help* them. To *do* something. To *know* something. To get, what do they say? 'To get on in the world.' How can I do that if I don't, if I fail? But I don't *understand*. I don't *understand*. I don't understand what anything means . . . and I walk around. From morning 'til night: with this one thought in my head. I'm *stupid*.

John   No one thinks you're stupid.

Carol   No? What am I . . . ?

John   I . . .

Carol   . . . what am I, then?

John   I think you're angry. Many people are. I have a *telephone* call that I have to make. And an *appointment*, which is rather *pressing*; though I sympathize with your concerns, and though I wish I had the time, this was not a previously scheduled meeting and I . . .

Carol   . . . you think I'm nothing . . .

John   . . . have an appointment with a *realtor*, and with my wife and . . .

Carol   You think that I'm stupid.

John   No. I certainly don't.

Carol   You said it.

John   No. I did not.

Carol   You did.

John   When?

Carol   . . . you . . .

John   No. I never did, or never would say that to a student, and . . .

Carol   You said, 'What can that mean?' (*Pause.*) 'What can that mean?" ... (*Pause.*)

John   ... and what did that mean to you ... ?

Carol   That meant I'm stupid. And I'll never learn. That's what that meant. And you're right.

John   ... I ...

Carol   But then. But then, what am I doing here ... ?

John   ... if you thought that I ...

Carol   ... when nobody wants me, and ...

John   ... if you interpreted ...

Carol   Nobody *tells* me anything. And I *sit* there ... in the *corner*. In the *back*. And everybody's talking about 'this' all the time. And 'concepts,' and 'precepts' and, and, and, and, and, WHAT IN THE WORLD ARE YOU *TALKING* ABOUT? And I read your book. And they said, 'Fine, go in that class.' Because you talked about responsibility to the young. I DON'T KNOW WHAT IT MEANS AND I'M *FAILING* ...

John   May ...

Carol   No, you're right. 'Oh, hell.' I failed. Flunk me out of it. It's garbage. Everything I do. 'The ideas contained in this work express the author's feelings.' That's right. That's right. I know I'm stupid. I know what I am. (*Pause.*) I know what I am, Professor. You don't have to tell me. (*Pause.*) It's pathetic. Isn't it?

John   ... Aha ... (*Pause.*) Sit down. Sit down. Please. (*Pause.*) Please sit down.

Carol   Why?

John   I want to talk to you.

Carol   Why?

John   Just sit down. (*Pause.*) Please. Sit down. Will you, please ... ? (*Pause. She does so.*) Thank you.

Carol   What?

John   I want to tell you something.

Carol   (*pause*)   What?

John   Well, I know what you're talking about.

Carol   No. You don't.

John   I think I do. (*Pause.*)

Carol   How can you?

John   I'll tell you a story about myself. (*Pause.*) Do you mind? (*Pause.*) I was raised to think myself stupid. That's what I want to tell you. (*Pause.*)

Carol   What do you mean?

John   Just what I said. I was brought up, and my earliest, and most persistent memories are of being told that I was stupid. 'You have such *intelligence*. Why must you behave so *stupidly*?' Or, 'Can't you *understand*? Can't you *understand*?' And I could *not* understand. I could *not* understand.

Carol   What?

John   The simplest problem. Was beyond me. It was a mystery.

Carol   What was a mystery?

John   How people learn. How *I* could learn. Which is what I've been speaking of in class. And of *course* you can't hear it. Carol. Of *course* you can't. (*Pause.*) I used to speak of 'real people,' and wonder what the *real* people did. The *real* people. Who were they? *They* were the people other than myself. The *good* people. The *capable* people. The people who could do the things, *I* could not do: learn, study, retain ... all that *garbage* – which is what I have been talking of in class, and that's *exactly* what I have been talking of – If you are told ... Listen to this. If the young child is told he cannot understand. Then he takes it as a *description* of himself. What am I? I am *that which can not understand*. And I saw you out there, when we were speaking of the concepts of . . .

Carol I can't understand any of them.

John Well, then, that's *my* fault. That's not your fault. And that is not verbiage. That's what I firmly hold to be the truth. And I am sorry, and I owe you an apology.

Carol Why?

John And I suppose that I have had some *things* on my mind. . . . We're buying a *house*, and . . .

Carol People said that you were stupid . . . ?

John Yes.

Carol When?

John I'll tell you when. Through my life. In my childhood; and, perhaps, they stopped. But I heard them continue.

Carol And what did they say?

John They said I was incompetent. Do you see? And when I'm tested the, the, the *feelings* of my youth about the *very subject of learning* come up. And I . . . I become, I feel 'unworthy,' and 'unprepared.' . . .

Carol . . . yes.

John . . . eh?

Carol . . . yes.

John And I feel that I must fail. (*Pause.*)

Carol . . . but then you *do* fail. (*Pause.*) You have to. (*Pause.*) Don't you?

John A *pilot.* Flying a plane. The pilot is flying the plane. He thinks: Oh, my *God*, my mind's been drifting! Oh, my God! What kind of a cursed imbecile am I, that I, with this so precious cargo of *Life* in my charge, would allow my attention to wander. Why was I born? How deluded are those who put their trust in me, . . . et cetera, so on, and he crashes the plane.

Carol (*pause*) He could just . . .

John That's right.

Carol He could say:

John My attention *wandered* for a moment . . .

Carol . . . uh huh . . .

John I had a *thought* I did not like . . . but now:

Carol . . . but now it's . . .

John That's what I'm telling you. It's time to put my attention . . . see: it is not: this is what I learned. It is Not Magic. Yes. Yes. *You.* You are going to be frightened. When faced with what may or may not be but which you are going to perceive as a test. You will become frightened. And you will say: 'I am incapable of . . .' and everything *in* you will think these two things. 'I must. But I can't.' And you will think: Why was I born to be the laughingstock of a world in which everyone is better than I? In which I am entitled to nothing. Where I can not learn.

Pause.

Carol Is that . . . (*Pause.*) Is that what I have . . . ?

John Well. I don't know if I'd put it that way. Listen: I'm talking to you as I'd talk to my son. Because that's what I'd like him to have that I never had. I'm talking to you the way I wish that someone had talked to me. I don't know how to do it, other than to be *personal*, . . . but . . .

Carol Why would you want to be personal with me?

John Well, you see? That's what I'm saying. We can only interpret the behaviour of others through the screen we . . . (*The phone rings.*) Through . . . (*To phone.*) Hello . . . ? (*To* **Carol**.) Through the screen we create. (*To phone.*) Hello. (*To* **Carol**.) Excuse me a moment. (*To phone.*) Hello? No, I can't talk nnn . . . I know I did. In a few . . . I'm . . . is he coming to the . . . yes. I talked to him. We'll meet you at the . . . No, because I'm with a *student*. It's going to be fff . . . This is important, too. I'm with a *student*, Jerry's going to . . . Listen: the sooner I get off, the sooner I'll be down, all right. I love you. Listen, listen, I said 'I love you,' it's going to work *out* with the, because I feel that it is, I'll be right down. All right? Well, then it's going to take as long as it takes. (*He hangs up.*) (*To* **Carol**.) I'm sorry.

Carol   What was that?

John   There are some problems, as there usually are, about the final agreements for the new house.

Carol   You're buying a new house.

John   That's right.

Carol   Because of your promotion.

John   Well, I suppose that that's right.

Carol   Why did you stay here with me?

John   Stay here.

Carol   Yes. When you should have gone.

John   Because I like you.

Carol   You like me.

John   Yes.

Carol   Why?

John   Why? Well? Perhaps we're similar. (*Pause.*) Yes. (*Pause.*)

Carol   You said 'everyone has problems.'

John   Everyone has problems.

Carol   Do they?

John   Certainly.

Carol   You do?

John   Yes.

Carol What are they?

John Well. (*Pause.*) Well, you're perfectly right. (*Pause.*) If we're going to take off the Artificial *Stricture*, of 'Teacher,' and 'Student,' why should *my* problems be any more a mystery than your own? Of *course* I have problems. As you saw.

Carol ... with what?

John With my *wife* ... with *work* ...

Carol With work?

John Yes. And, and, perhaps my problems are, do you see? *Similar* to yours.

Carol Would you tell me?

John All right. (*Pause.*) I came *late* to teaching. And I found it Artificial. The notion of 'I know and you do not'; and I saw an *exploitation* in the education process. I told you. I hated school, I hated teachers. I hated everyone who was in the position of a 'boss' because I *knew* – I didn't *think*, mind you, I *knew* I was going to fail. Because I was a fuckup. I was just no goddamned good. When I ... late in life ... (*Pause.*) When I *got out from under* ... when I worked my way out of the need to fail. When I ...

Carol How do you do that? (*Pause.*)

John You have to look at what you are, and what you feel, and how you act. And, finally, you have to look at how you act. And say: If that's what I *did*, that must be how I think of myself.

Carol I don't understand.

John If I fail all the time, it must be that I think of myself as a failure. If I do not want to think of myself as a failure, perhaps I should begin by *succeeding* now and again. Look. The tests, you see, which you encounter, in school, in college, in life, were designed, in the most part, for idiots. *By* idiots. There is no need to fail at them. They are not a test of your worth. They are a test of your ability to retain and spout back misinformation. Of *course* you fail them. They're *nonsense*. And I ...

Carol ... no ...

John Yes. They're *garbage*. They're a *joke*. Look at me. Look at me. The Tenure Committee. The Tenure Committee. Come to judge me. The Bad Tenure Committee.

The 'Test.' Do you see? They put me to the test. Why, they had people voting on me I wouldn't employ to wax my car. And yet, I go before the Great Tenure Committee, and I have an urge, to *vomit*, to, to, to puke my *badness* on the table, to show them: 'I'm no good. Why would you pick *me*?'

Carol They granted you tenure.

John Oh no, they announced it, but they haven't *signed*. Do you see? 'At any moment ...'

Carol ... mmm ...

John 'They might not *sign*' ... I might not ... the *house* might not go through ... Eh? Eh? They'll find out my 'dark secret.' (*Pause.*)

Carol ... what is it ... ?

John There *isn't* one. But *they* will find an index of my badness ...

Carol Index?

John A '... pointer.' A 'Pointer.' You see? Do you see? I *understand* you. I. Know. That. Feeling. Am I entitled to my job, and my nice *home*, and my *wife*, and my *family*, and so on. This is what I'm saying: That theory of education which, that *theory*:

Carol I ... I ... (*Pause.*)

John What?

Carol I ...

John What?

Carol I want to know about my grade. (*Long pause.*)

John Of course you do.

Carol Is that bad?

John No.

Carol Is it bad that I asked you that?

John No.

Carol Did I upset you?

John No. And I apologize. Of *course* you want to know about your grade. And, of course, you can't concentrate on anyth . . . (*The telephone starts to ring.*) Wait a moment.

Carol I should go.

John I'll make you a deal.

Carol No, you have to . . .

John Let it ring. I'll make you a deal. You stay here. We'll start the whole course over. I'm going to say it was not you, it was I who was not paying attention. We'll start the whole course over. Your grade is an 'A.' Your final grade is an 'A.' (*The phone stops ringing.*)

Carol But the class is only half over . . .

John (*simultaneously with 'over'*) Your grade for the whole term is an 'A.' If you will come back and meet with me. A few more times. Your grade's an 'A.' Forget about the paper. You didn't like it, you didn't like writing it. It's not important. What's important is that I awake your interest, if I can, and that I answer your questions. Let's start over. (*Pause.*)

Carol Over. With what?

John Say this is the beginning.

Carol The beginning.

John Yes.

Carol Of what?

John Of the class.

Carol But we can't start over.

John I say we can. (*Pause.*) I say we can.

Carol But I don't believe it.

John Yes, I know that. But it's true. What is The Class but you and me? (*Pause.*)

Carol There are rules.

John Well. We'll break them.

Carol How can we?

John We won't tell anybody.

Carol Is that all right?

John I say that it's fine.

Carol Why would you do this for me?

John I like you. Is that so difficult for you to . . .

Carol Um . . .

John There's no one here but you and me. (*Pause.*)

Carol All right. I did not understand. When you referred . . .

John All right, yes?

Carol When you referred to hazing.

John Hazing.

Carol You wrote, in your book. About the comparative . . . the comparative . . . (*She checks her notes.*)

John Are you checking your notes . . . ?

Carol Yes.

John Tell me in your own . . .

Carol I want to make sure that I have it right.

John No. Of course. You want to be exact.

Carol I want to know everything that went on.

John . . . that's good.

Carol . . . so I . . .

John That's very good. But I was suggesting, many times, that that which we wish to retain is retained oftentimes, I think, *better* with less expenditure of effort.

Carol (*of notes*) Here it is: you wrote of *hazing*.

John . . . that's correct. Now: I said 'hazing.' It means ritualized annoyance. We shove this book at you, we read it. Now, you say you've read it? I think that you're *lying*. I'll *grill* you, and when I find you've lied, you'll be disgraced, and your life will be ruined. It's a sick game. Why do we do it? Does it educate? In no sense. Well, then, what is higher education? It is something-other-than-useful.

Carol What is 'something-other-than-useful?'

John It has become a ritual, it has become an article of faith. That all must be subjected to, or to put it differently, that all are entitled to Higher Education. And my point . . .

Carol You disagree with that?

John Well, let's address that. What do you think?

Carol I don't know.

John What do you think, though? (*Pause.*)

Carol I don't know.

John I spoke of it in class. Do you remember my example?

Carol Justice.

John Yes. Can you repeat it to me? (*She looks down at her* *notebook.*) Without your notes? I ask you as a favor to me, so that I can see if my idea was interesting.

Carol You said 'justice' . . .

John Yes?

Carol . . . that all are entitled . . . (*Pause.*) I . . . I . . . I . . .

John Yes. To a speedy trial. To a fair trial. But they needn't be given a trial *at all* unless they stand accused. Eh? Justice is their right, should they choose to avail themselves of it, they should have a fair trial. It does not follow, of necessity, a person's life is incomplete without a trial in it. Do you see?

My point is a confusion between equity and *utility* arose. So we confound the *usefulness* of higher education with our, granted, right to equal access to the same. We, in effect, create a *prejudice* toward it, completely independent of . . .

Carol . . . that it is prejudice that we should go to school?

John Exactly. (*Pause.*)

Carol How can you say that? How . . .

John Good. Good. *Good.* That's right! Speak up! What is a prejudice? An unreasoned belief. We are all subject to it. none of us is not. When it is threatened, or opposed, we feel anger, and feel, do we not? As you do now. Do you not? Good.

Carol . . . but how can you . . .

John . . . let us examine. Good.

Carol How . . .

John Good. Good. When . . .

Carol I'M SPEAKING . . . (*Pause.*)

John I'm sorry.

Carol How can you . . .

John   ... I beg your pardon.

Carol   That's all right.

John   I beg your pardon.

Carol   That's all right.

John   I'm sorry I interrupted you.

Carol   That's all right.

John   You were saying?

Carol   I was saying ... I was saying ... (*She checks her notes.*) How can you say in a class. Say in a college class, that college education is prejudice?

John   I said that our predilection for it ...

Carol   Predilection ...

John   ... you know what that means.

Carol   Does it mean 'liking'?

John   Yes.

Carol   But how can you say that? That College ...

John   ... that's my *job*, don't you know.

Carol   What is?

John   To provoke you.

Carol   No.

John   Oh. Yes, though.

Carol   To provoke me?

John   That's right.

Carol   To make me mad?

John   That's right. To force you ...

Carol   ... to make me mad is your job?

John   To force you to ... listen: (*Pause.*) Ah. (*Pause.*) When

I was young somebody told me, are you ready, the rich copulate less often than the poor. But when they do, they take more of their clothes off. Years. Years, mind you, I would compare experiences of my own to this dictum, saying, aha, this fits the norm, or ah, this is a variation from it. What did it mean? Nothing. It was some jerk thing, some school kid told me that took up room inside my head. (*Pause.*)

Somebody told *you*, and you hold it as an article of faith, that higher education is an unassailable good. This notion is so dear to you that when I question it you become angry. Good. Good, I say. Are not those the very things which we should question? I say college education, since the war, has become so a matter of course, and such a fashionable necessity, for those either of or aspiring *to* to the new vast middle class, that we *espouse* it, as a matter of right, and have ceased to ask, 'What is it good for?' (*Pause.*)

What might be some reasons for pursuit of higher education?
One: A love of learning.
Two: The wish for mastery of a skill.
Three: For economic betterment.
(*Stops. Makes a note.*)

Carol I'm keeping you.

John One moment. I have to make a note . . .

Carol It's something that I said?

John No, we're buying a house.

Carol You're buying the new house.

John To go with the tenure. That's right. Nice *house*, close to the *private school* . . . (*He continues making his note.*) . . . We were talking of economic *betterment* (**Carol** *writes in her notebook.*) . . . I was thinking of the School Tax. (*He continues writing.*) (*To himself.*) . . . *where is it written* that I have to send my child to public school. . . . Is it a law that I have to improve the City Schools at the expense of my own interest? And, is this not simply *The White Man's Burden*? Good. And (*Looks up to* **Carol**.) . . . does this interest you?

Carol   No. I'm taking notes . . .

John   You don't have to take notes, you know, you can just listen.

Carol   I want to make sure I remember it. (*Pause.*)

John   I'm not lecturing you, I'm just trying to tell you some things I think.

Carol   What do you think?

John   Should all kids go to college? *Why* . . .

Carol (*pause*)   To learn.

John   But if he does not learn.

Carol   If the child does not learn?

John   Then why is he in college? Because he was told it was his 'right'?

Carol   Some might find college instructive.

John   I would hope so.

Carol   But how do they feel? Being told they are wasting their time?

John   I don't think I'm telling them that.

Carol   You said that education was 'prolonged and systematic hazing.'

John   Yes. It can be so.

Carol   . . . if education is so *bad*, why do you do it?

John   I do it because I love it. (*Pause.*) Let's . . . I suggest you look at the demographics, wage-earning capacity, college- and non-college-educated men and women, 1855 to 1980, and let's see if we can wring some worth from the statistics. Eh? And . . .

Carol   No.

John   What?

Carol   I can't understand them.

John   . . . you . . . ?

Carol   . . . the 'charts.' The *Concepts*, the . . .

John   'Charts' are simply . . .

Carol   When I leave here . . .

John   Charts, do you see . . .

Carol   No, I can't . . .

John   You can, though.

Carol   NO, NO – I DON'T UNDERSTAND. DO YOU SEE??? I DON'T *UNDERSTAND* . . .

John   What?

Carol   *Any* of it. *Any* of it. I'm *smiling* in class, I'm *smiling*, the whole time. What are you *talking* about? What is everyone *talking* about? I don't *understand*. I don't know what it *means*. I don't know what it means to *be* here . . . you tell me I'm intelligent, and then you tell me I should not be *here*, what do you *want* with me? What does it *mean?* Who should I *listen* to . . . I . . .

He goes over to her and puts his arm around her shoulder.

NO! (*She walks away from him.*)

John   Sshhhh.

Carol   No, I don't under . . .

John   Sshhhhh.

Carol   I don't know what you're *saying* . . .

John   Sshhhhh. It's all right.

Carol   . . . I have no . . .

John   Sshhhhh. Sshhhhh. Let it go a moment. (*Pause.*) Sshhhhh . . . let it go. (*Pause.*) Just let it go. (*Pause.*) Just let

it go. It's all right. (*Pause.*) Sshhhh. (*Pause.*) I understand
. . . (*Pause.*) What do you feel?

Carol I feel bad.

John I know. It's all right.

Carol I . . . (*Pause.*)

John What?

Carol I . . .

John What? Tell me.

Carol I don't understand you.

John I know. It's all right.

Carol I . . .

John What? (*Pause.*) What? *Tell* me.

Carol I can't tell you.

John No, you must.

Carol I can't.

John No. Tell me. (*Pause.*)

Carol I'm bad. (*Pause.*) Oh, God. (*Pause.*)

John It's all right.

Carol I'm . . .

John It's all right.

Carol I can't talk about this.

John It's all right. Tell me.

Carol Why do you want to know this?

John I don't want to know. I want to know whatever
you . . .

Carol I always . . .

John . . . good . . .

Carol I always ... all my life ... I have never told anyone this ...

John Yes. Go on. (*Pause.*) Go on.

Carol All of my life ... (*The phone rings.*) (*Pause.* **John** *goes to the phone and picks it up.*)

John (*into phone*) I can't talk now. (*Pause.*) What? (*Pause.*) Hmm. (*Pause.*) All right, I ... I. Can't. Talk. Now. No, no, no, I *Know* I did, but ... What? Hello. What? She *what?* She *can't*, she said the agreement is void? How, how is the agreement *void? That's Our House.*

I have the *paper;* when we come down, next week, with the payment, and the paper, that house is ... wait, wait, wait, wait, wait, wait, wait: Did Jerry ... is Jerry there? (*Pause.*) Is *she* there ...? Does she have a *lawyer* ...? How the *hell,* how the *Hell.* That is ... it's a question, you said, of the *easement.* I don't underst ... it's not the *whole agreement.* It's just the *easement,* why would she? Put, put, put, *Jerry* on. (*Pause.*) Jer, *Jerry:* What the *Hell* ... that's my *house.* That's ... Well, I'm, no, no, no, I'm *not* coming ddd ... List, *Listen, screw* her. You *tell* her. You, listen: I want you to take *Grace,* you take Grace, and get out of that house. You *leave* her there. Her and her lawyer, and you *tell* them, we'll see them in court next ... no. No. Leave her there, leave her to *stew* in it: You tell her, we're *getting* that house, and we are going to ... No. I'm *not* coming down. I'll be damned if I'll sit in the same rrr ... the next, you tell her the next time I *see* her is in court ... I ... (*Pause.*) What? (*Pause.*) What? I don't understand. (*Pause.*) Well, what about the house? (*Pause.*) There isn't any problem with the hhh ... (*Pause.*) No, no, no, that's all right. All ri ... All right ... (*Pause.*) Of course. Tha ... Thank you. No, I will. Right away. (*He hangs up.*) (*Pause.*)

Carol What is it? (*Pause.*)

John It's a surprise party.

Carol It is.

John　Yes.

Carol　A party for you.

John　Yes.

Carol　Is it your birthday?

John　No.

Carol　What is it?

John　The tenure announcement.

Carol　The tenure announcement.

John　They're throwing a party for us in our new house.

Carol　Your new house.

John　The house that we're buying.

Carol　You have to go.

John　It seems that I do.

Carol (*pause*)　They're proud of you.

John　Well, there are those who would say it's a form of aggression.

Carol　What is?

John　A surprise.

Act Two

John *and* **Carol** *seated across the desk from each other.*

John You see, (*Pause.*) I love to teach. And flatter myself I am *skilled* at it. And I love the, the aspect of *performance*. I think I must confess that.

When I found I loved to teach I swore that I would not become that cold, rigid automaton of an instructor which I had encountered as a child.

Now, I was not unconscious that it was given me to err upon the other side. And, so, I asked and *ask* myself if I engaged in heterodoxy, I will not say 'gratuitously' for I do not care to posit orthodoxy as a given good – but, 'to the detriment of, of my students.' (*Pause.*)

As I said. When the possibility of tenure opened, and, of course, I'd long pursued it, I was, of course *happy*, and *covetous* of it.

I asked myself if I was wrong to covet it. And thought about it long, and, I hope, truthfully, and saw in myself several things in, I think, no particular order. (*Pause.*)

That I *would* pursue it. That I *desired* it, that I was not pure of longing for security, and that that, perhaps, was not reprehensible in me. That I had duties *beyond* the school, and that my duty to my home, for instance, was, or should be, if it were not, of an equal weight. That tenure, and security, and yes, and *comfort*, were not, of themselves, to be scorned; and were even worthy of honorable pursuit. And that it was given me. Here, in this place, which I enjoy, and in which I find comfort, to assure myself of – as far as it rests in The Material – a continuation of that joy and comfort. In exchange for what? Teaching. Which I love.

What was the price of this security? To obtain *tenure*. Which tenure the committee is in the process of granting me. And on the basis of which I contracted to purchase a house.

Now, as you don't have your own family, at this point, you
may not know what that means. But to me it is important.
A home. A Good Home. To raise my family. Now: The
Tenure Committee will meet. This is the process, and a
good process. Under which the school has functioned for
quite a long time. They will meet, and hear your complaint
– which you have the right to make; and they will dismiss
it. They will *dismiss* your complaint; and, in the intervening
period, I will lose my house. I will not be able to close on
my house. I will lose my *deposit*, and the home I'd picked
out for my wife and son will go by the boards. Now: I see
I have angered you. I understand your anger at teachers. I
was angry with mine. I felt hurt and humiliated by them.
Which is one of the reasons that I went into education.

Carol What do you want of me?

John (*pause*) I was hurt. When I received the report. Of
the tenure committee. I was shocked. And I was hurt. No,
I don't mean to subject you to my weak sensibilities. All
right. Finally, I didn't understand. Then I thought: is it not
always at those points at which we reckon ourselves
unassailable that we are most vulnerable and . . . (*Pause.*)
Yes. All right. You find me pedantic. Yes. I am. By nature,
by *birth*, by profession, I don't know . . . I'm always looking
for a *paradigm* for . . .

Carol I don't know what a paradigm is.

John It's a model.

Carol Then why can't you use that word? (*Pause.*)

John If it is important to you. Yes, all right. I was
looking for a model. To continue: I feel that one point . . .

Carol I . . .

John One second . . . upon which I am unassailable is
my unflinching concern for my students' dignity. I asked
you here to . . . in the spirit of *investigation*, to ask you . . . to
ask . . . (*Pause.*) What have I done to you? (*Pause.*) And, and,
I suppose, how I can make amends. Can we not settle this

now? It's pointless, really, and I want to know.

Carol   What you can do to force me to retract?

John   That is not what I meant at all.

Carol   To bribe me, to convince me . . .

John   . . . No.

Carol   To retract . . .

John   That is not what I meant at all. I think that you know it is not.

Carol   That is not what I know. I *wish* I . . .

John   I do not want to . . . you wish what?

Carol   No, you said what amends can you make. To force me to retract.

John   That is not what I said.

Carol   I have my notes.

John   Look. Look. The Stoics say . . .

Carol   The Stoics?

John   The Stoical Philosophers say if you remove the phrase 'I have been injured,' you have removed the injury. Now: Think: I know that you're upset. Just tell me. Literally. Literally: what wrong have I done you?

Carol   Whatever you have done to me – to the extent that you've done it to *me*, do you know, rather than to me as a *student*, and, so, to the student body, is contained in my report. To the tenure committee.

John   Well, all right. (*Pause.*) Let's see. (*He reads.*) I find that I am sexist. That I am *elitist*. I'm not sure I know what that means, other than it's a derogatory word, meaning 'bad.' That I . . . That I insist on wasting time, in nonprescribed, in self-aggrandizing and theatrical *diversions* from the prescribed *text* . . . that these have taken both sexist and pornographic forms . . . here we find listed . . .

(*Pause.*) Here we find listed . . . instances '. . . closeted with a student' . . . 'Told a rambling, sexually explicit story, in which the frequency and attitudes of fornication of the poor and rich are, it would seem, the central point . . . moved to *embrace* said student and . . . all part of a pattern . . .' (*Pause.*)

(*He reads.*) That I used the phrase 'The White Man's Burden' . . . that I told you how I'd asked you to my room because I quote like you. (*Pause.*)

(*He reads.*) 'He said he "liked" me. That he "liked being with me." He'd let me write my examination paper over, if I could come back oftener to see him in his office.' (*Pause.*) (*To* **Carol**.) It's *ludicrous*. Don't you know that? It's not *necessary*. It's going to *humiliate* you, and it's going to cost me my *house*, and . . .

Carol It's '*ludicrous* . . .'?

John *picks up the report and reads again.*

John 'He told me he had problems with his wife; and that he wanted to take off the artificial stricture of Teacher and Student. He put his arm around me . . .'

Carol Do you deny it? Can you deny it . . . ? Do you see? (*Pause.*) Don't you see? You don't see, do you?

John I don't see . . .

Carol You think, you think you can deny that these things happened; or, if they *did*, if they *did*, that they meant what you *said* they meant. Don't you see? You drag me in here, you drag us, to listen to you 'go on'; and 'go on' about this, or that, or we don't 'express' ourselves very well. We don't say what we mean. Don't we? Don't we? We *do* say what we mean. And you say that 'I don't understand you . . .': Then *you* . . . (*Points.*)

John 'Consult the Report'?

Carol . . . that's right.

John You see. You see. Can't you. . . . You see what I'm saying? Can't you tell me in your own words?

Carol Those are my own words. (*Pause.*)

John (*reads*) 'He told me that if I would stay alone with him in his office, he would change my grade to an A.' (*To* **Carol**.) What have I done to you? Oh. My God, are you so hurt?

Carol What I 'feel' is irrelevant. (*Pause.*)

John Do you know that I tried to help you?

Carol What I know I have reported.

John I would like to help you now. I would. Before this escalates.

Carol (*simultaneously with* 'escalates') You see. I don't think that I need your help. I don't think I need anything you have.

John I feel . . .

Carol I don't *care* what you feel. Do you see? DO YOU SEE? You can't *do* that anymore. You. Do. Not. Have. The. Power. Did you misuse it? *Someone* did. Are you part of that group? *Yes. Yes.* You Are. You've *done* these things. And to say, and to say, 'Oh. Let me help you with your problem . . .'

John Yes. I understand. I understand. You're *hurt*. You're *angry*. Yes. I think your *anger* is *betraying* you. Down a path which helps no one.

Carol I don't *care* what you think.

John You don't? (*Pause.*) But you talk of *rights*. Don't you see? *I* have rights too. Do you see? I have a *house* . . . part of the *real* world; and The Tenure Committee, Good Men and True . . .

Carol . . . Professor . . .

John . . . Please: *Also* part of that world: you understand? This is my *life*. I'm not a *bogeyman*. I don't 'stand' for something, I . . .

Carol   ... Professor ...

John   ... I ...

Carol   Professor. I came here as a *favor*. At your personal request. Perhaps I should not have done so. But I did. On my behalf, and on behalf of my group. And you speak of the tenure committee, one of whose members is a woman, as you know. And though you might call it Good Fun, or An Historical Phrase, or An Oversight, or, All of the Above, to refer to the committee as Good Men and True, it is a demeaning remark. It is a sexist remark, and to overlook it is to countenance continuation of that method of thought. It's a remark ...

John   OH COME ON. Come on. ... Sufficient to deprive a family of ...

Carol   Sufficient? Sufficient? Sufficient? Yes. It is a *fact* ... and that story, which I quote, is *vile* and *classist*, and *manipulative* and *pornographic*. It ...

John   ... it's pornographic ... ?

Carol   What gives you the *right*. Yes. To speak to a *woman* in your private ... Yes. Yes. I'm sorry. I'm sorry. You feel yourself empowered ... you say so yourself. To *strut*. To *posture*. To 'perform.' To 'Call me in here ...' Eh? You say that higher education is a joke. And treat it as such, you *treat* it as such. And *confess* to a taste to play the *Patriarch* in your class. To grant *this*. To deny *that*. To embrace your students.

John   How can you assert. How can you stand there and ...

Carol   How can you *deny* it. You did it to me. *Here*. You *did*. ... You *confess*. You love the Power. To *deviate*. To *invent*, to transgress ... to *transgress* whatever norms have been established for us. And you think it's charming to 'question' in yourself this taste to mock and destroy. But you should question it. Professor. And you pick those things which you feel *advance* you: publication, *tenure*, and the steps

to get them you call 'harmless rituals.' And you perform
those steps. Although you say it is hypocrisy. But to the
aspirations of your students. Of *hardworking students*, who
come here, who *slave* to come here – you have no idea
what it cost me to come to this school – you *mock* us. You
call education 'hazing,' and from your so-protected, so-elitist
seat you hold our confusion as a *joke*, and our hopes and
efforts with it. Then you sit there and say 'what have I
done?' and ask me to understand that *you* have aspirations
too. But I tell you. I tell you. That you are vile. And that
you are exploitative. And if you possess one ounce of that
inner honesty you describe in your book, you can look in
yourself and see those things that I see. And you can find
revulsion equal to my own. Good day. (*She prepares to leave
the room.*)

John   Wait a second, will you, just one moment. (*Pause.*)
Nice day today.

Carol   What?

John   You said 'Good day.' I think that it is a nice day
today.

Carol   *Is* it?

John   Yes, I think it is.

Carol   And why is that important?

John   Because it is the essence of all human
communication. I say something conventional, you respond,
and the information we exchange is not about the
'weather,' but that we both agree to converse. In effect, we
agree that we are both human. (*Pause.*)

I'm not a . . . 'exploiter,' and you're not a . . . 'deranged,'
what? *Revolutionary* . . . that we may, that we may have . . .
positions, and that we may have . . . desires, which are in
conflict, but that we're just human. (*Pause.*) That means that
sometimes we're *imperfect*. (*Pause.*) Often we're in conflict . . .
(*Pause.*) *Much* of what we do, you're right, in the name of
'principles' is *self-serving* . . . much of what we do is

conventional. (*Pause.*) You're right. (*Pause.*) You said you came in the class because you wanted to learn about *education.* I don't know that I can teach you about education. But I know that I can tell you what I *think* about education, and then *you* decide. And you don't have to fight with me. *I'm* not the subject. (*Pause.*) And where I'm *wrong* ... perhaps it's not your job to 'fix' me. I don't want to fix *you.* I would like to tell you what I *think,* because that *is* my job, conventional as it is, and flawed as I may be. And then, if you can show me some better *form,* then we can proceed from there. But, just like 'nice day, isn't it ... ?' I don't think we can proceed until we accept that each of us is human. (*Pause.*) And we still can have difficulties. We *will* have them ... that's all right too. (*Pause.*) Now:

Carol   ... wait ...

John   Yes. I want to hear it.

Carol   ... the ...

John   Yes. Tell me frankly.

Carol   ... my position ...

John   I want to hear it. In your own words. What you want. And what you feel.

Carol   ... I ...

John   ... yes ...

Carol   My Group.

John   Your 'Group' ... ? (*Pause.*)

Carol   The people I've been talking to ...

John   There's no shame in that. Everybody needs advisers. Everyone needs to expose themselves. To various points of view. It's not wrong. It's essential. Good. Good. Now: You and I ... (*The phone rings.*)
You and I ...
(*He hesitates for a moment, and then picks it up.*) (*Into phone.*)
Hello. (*Pause.*) Um ... no, I know they do. (*Pause.*) I know

she does. Tell her that I ... can I call you back? ... Then tell her that I think it's going to be fine. (*Pause.*) Tell her just, just hold on, I'll ... can I get back to you? ... Well ... no, no, no, we're *taking* the house ... we're ... no, no, nn ... no, she will nnn, it's not a *question* of refunding the dep ... no ... it's not a *question* of the deposit ... will you call Jerry? Babe, baby, will you just call Jerry? Tell him, nnn ... tell him they, well, they're to keep the deposit, because the deal, be ... because the deal is going to go *through* ... because I know ... be ... will you please? Just *trust* me. Be ... well, I'm dealing with the complaint. Yes. Right *Now*. Which is why I ... yes, no, no, it's really, I can't *talk* about it now. Call Jerry, and I can't talk now. Ff ... fine. Gg ... good-bye. (*Hangs up.*) (*Pause.*) I'm sorry we were interrupted.

Carol No ...

John I ... I was saying.

Carol You said that we should agree to talk about my complaint.

John That's correct.

Carol But we *are* talking about it.

John Well, that's correct too. You see? This is the *gist* of education.

Carol No, no. I mean, we're talking about it at the Tenure Committee Hearing. (*Pause.*)

John Yes, but I'm saying: we can talk about it *now*, as easily as ...

Carol No. I think that we should stick to the process ...

John ... wait a ...

Carol ... the 'conventional' process. As you said. (*She gets up.*) And you're right, I'm sorry if I was, um, if I was 'discourteous' to you. You're right.

John Wait, wait a ...

Carol I really should go.

John Now, look, granted. I have an interest. In the status quo. All right? Everyone does. But what I'm saying is that the *committee* . . .

Carol Professor, you're right. Just don't impinge on me. We'll take our differences, and . . .

John You're going to make a . . . look, look, look, you're going to . . .

Carol I shouldn't have come here. They told me . . .

John One moment. No. No. There are *norms*, here, and there's no reason. Look: I'm trying to *save* you . . .

Carol No one *asked* you to . . . you're trying to save *me*? Do me the courtesy to . . .

John I *am* doing you the courtesy. I'm talking *straight* to you. We can settle this *now*. And I want you to sit *down* and . . .

Carol You must excuse me . . . (*She starts to leave the room.*)

John Sit down, it seems we each have a . . . Wait one moment. Wait one moment . . . just do me the courtesy to . . .

He restrains her from leaving.

Carol LET ME GO.

John I have no desire to *hold* you, I just want to *talk* to you . . .

Carol LET ME GO. LET ME GO. WOULD SOMEBODY *HELP* ME? WOULD SOMEBODY *HELP* ME PLEASE . . . ?

Act Three

At rise, **Carol** *and* **John** *are seated.*

John I have asked you here. (*Pause.*) I have asked you here against, against my . . .

Carol I was most surprised you asked me.

John . . . against my better *judgment*, against . . .

Carol I was most surprised . . .

John . . . against the . . . yes. I'm sure.

Carol . . . If you would like me to leave, I'll leave. I'll go right now . . . (*She rises.*)

John Let us begin *correctly*, may we? I feel . . .

Carol That is what I wished to do. That's why I came here, but now . . .

John . . . I feel . . .

Carol But now perhaps you'd like me to leave . . .

John I don't want you to leave. I asked you to come . . .

Carol I didn't have to come here.

John No. (*Pause.*) Thank you.

Carol All right. (*Pause.*) (*She sits down.*)

John Although I feel that it *profits*, it would *profit* you something, to . . .

Carol . . . what I . . .

John If you would hear me out, if you would hear me out.

Carol I came here to, the court officers told me not to come.

John . . . the 'court' officers . . . ?

Carol   I was shocked that you asked.

John   . . . wait . . .

Carol   Yes. But I did *not* come here to hear what it 'profits' me.

John   The 'court' officers . . .

Carol   . . . no, no, perhaps I should leave . . . (*She gets up.*)

John   Wait.

Carol   No. I shouldn't have . . .

John   . . . wait. Wait. Wait a moment.

Carol   Yes? What is it you want? (*Pause.*) What is it you want?

John   I'd like you to stay.

Carol   You want me to stay.

John   Yes.

Carol   You do.

John   Yes. (*Pause.*) Yes. I would like to have you hear me out. If you would. (*Pause.*) Would you please? If you would do that I would be in your debt. (*Pause.*) (*She sits.*) Thank You. (*Pause.*)

Carol   What is it you wish to tell me?

John   All right. I cannot . . . (*Pause.*) I cannot help but feel you are owed an apology. (*Pause.*) (*Of papers in his hands.*) I have read. (*Pause.*) And reread these accusations.

Carol   What 'accusations'?

John   The, the tenure comm . . . what other accusations . . . ?

Carol   The tenure committee . . . ?

John   Yes.

Carol   Excuse me, but those are not accusations. They

have been *proved*. They are facts.

John   . . . I . . .

Carol   No. Those are not 'accusations.'

John   . . . those?

Carol   . . . the committee (*The phone starts to ring.*) the committee has . . .

John   . . . All right . . .

Carol   . . . those are not accusations. The Tenure Committee.

John   ALL RIGHT. ALL RIGHT. ALL RIGHT. (*He picks up the phone.*) Hello. Yes. No. I'm here. Tell Mister . . . No, I can't talk to him now . . . I'm sure he has, but I'm fff . . . I know . . . No, I have no time t . . . tell Mister . . . tell Mist . . . tell Jerry that I'm *fine* and that I'll call him right aw . . . (*Pause.*) My wife . . . Yes. I'm sure she has. Yes, thank you. Yes, I'll call her too. I cannot talk to you now. (*He hangs up.*) (*Pause.*) All right. It was good of you to come. Thank you. I have studied. I have spent some time studying the indictment.

Carol   You will have to explain that word to me.

John   An 'indictment' . . .

Carol   Yes.

John   Is a 'bill of particulars.' A . . .

Carol   All right. Yes.

John   In which is alleged . . .

Carol   No. I cannot allow that. I cannot allow that. Nothing is alleged. Everything is proved . . .

John   Please, wait a sec . . .

Carol   I cannot *come* to allow . . .

John   If I may . . . If I may, from whatever you feel is 'established,' by . . .

Carol   The issue here is not what I 'feel.' It is not my
'feelings,' but the feelings of women. And men. Your
superiors, who've been 'polled,' do you see? To whom
evidence has been presented, who have *ruled*, do you see?
Who have weighed the testimony and the evidence, and
have *ruled*, do you see? That you are *negligent*. That you are
guilty, that you are found *wanting*, and in *error*; and are *not*,
for the reasons so-told, to be given tenure. That you are to
be disciplined. For facts. For *facts*. Not 'alleged,' what is the
word? But *proved*. Do you see? *By your own actions*.

That is what the tenure committee has said. That is what
my lawyer said. For what you did in class. For what you
did *in this office*.

John   They're going to discharge me.

Carol   As full well they should. You don't understand?
You're angry? What has *led* you to this place? Not your
sex. Not your race. Not your class. YOUR OWN
ACTIONS. And you're *angry*. You *ask* me here. What *do*
you want? You want to 'charm' me. You want to
'convince' me. You want me to recant. I will *not* recant.
Why should I . . . ? What I say is right. You tell me, you
are going to tell me that you have a wife and child. You
are going to say that you have a career and that you've
worked for twenty years for this. Do you know what you've
worked for? *Power*. For *power*. Do you understand? And you
sit there, and you tell me *stories*. About your *house*, about all
the private *schools*, and about *privilege*, and how you are
entitled. To *buy*, to *spend*, to *mock*, to *summon*. All your
stories. All your silly weak *guilt*, it's all about *privilege*; and
you won't know it. Don't you see? You worked twenty
years for the right to *insult* me. And you feel entitled to be
paid for it. Your Home. Your Wife . . . Your sweet 'deposit'
on your house . . .

John   Don't you have feelings?

Carol   That's my point. You see? Don't you have
feelings? Your final argument. What is it that has no
feelings. *Animals*. I don't take your side, you question if I'm

Human.

John Don't you have feelings?

Carol I have a responsibility. I . . .

John . . . to . . . ?

Carol To? This institution. To the *students*. To my *group*.

John . . . your 'group.' . . .

Carol Because I speak, yes, not for myself. But for the
group; for those who suffer what I suffer. On behalf of
whom, even if I, were, inclined, to what, forgive? Forget?
What? Overlook your . . .

John . . . my behavior?

Carol . . . it would be wrong.

John Even if you were inclined to 'forgive' me.

Carol It would be wrong.

John And what would transpire.

Carol Transpire?

John Yes.

Carol 'Happen?'

John Yes.

Carol Then *say* it. For Christ's sake. Who the *hell* do you
think that you are? You want a post. You want unlimited
power. To do and to say what you want. As it pleases you
– Testing, Questioning, Flirting . . .

John I never . . .

Carol Excuse me, one moment, will you?

She reads from her notes.

The twelfth: 'Have a good day, dear.'
The fifteenth: 'Now, don't *you* look fetching . . .'
April seventeenth: 'If you girls would come over here . . .' I

saw you. I saw you, Professor. For two semesters sit there, stand there and exploit our, as you thought, 'paternal prerogative,' and what is that but rape; I swear to God. You asked me in here to explain something to me, as a child, that I did not understand. But I came to explain something to you. You Are Not God. You ask me why I came? I came here to instruct you.

She produces his book.

And your book? You think you're going to show me some 'light'? You '*maverick*.' Outside of tradition. No, no, (*She reads from the book's liner notes.*) '*of* that fine tradition of *inquiry*. Of Polite *skepticism*' . . . and you say you believe in free intellectual discourse. YOU BELIEVE IN NOTHING. YOU BELIEVE IN NOTHING AT ALL.

John   I believe in freedom of thought.

Carol   Isn't that fine. *Do* you?

John   Yes. I do.

Carol   Then why do you question, for one moment, the committee's decision refusing your tenure? Why do you question your suspension? You believe in what *you call* freedom of thought. Then, fine. *You* believe in freedom-of-thought *and* a home, and, *and* prerogatives for your kid, *and* tenure. And I'm going to tell you. You believe *not* in 'freedom of thought,' but in an elitist, in, in a protected hierarchy which rewards you. And for whom you are the clown. And you mock and exploit the system which pays your rent. You're wrong. I'm not wrong. You're wrong. You think that I'm full of hatred. I know what you think I am.

John   Do you?

Carol   You think I'm a, of course I do. You think I am a frightened, repressed, confused, I don't know, abandoned young thing of some doubtful sexuality, who wants, power and revenge. (*Pause.*) *Don't* you? (*Pause.*)

John   Yes. I do. (*Pause.*)

Carol Isn't that better? And I feel that that is the first moment which you've treated me with respect. For you told me the truth. (*Pause.*) I did not come here, as you are assured, to gloat. Why would I want to gloat? I've profited nothing from your, your, as you say, your 'misfortune.' I came here, as you did me the honor to *ask* me here, I came here to *tell* you something.

Pause.

That I think ... that I think you've been wrong. That I think you've been terribly wrong. Do you hate me now? (*Pause.*)

John Yes.

Carol Why do you hate me? Because you think me wrong? No. Because I have, you think, *power* over you. Listen to me. Listen to me, Professor. (*Pause.*) It is the power that you hate. So deeply that, that any atmosphere of free discussion is impossible. It's not 'unlikely.' It's *impossible.* Isn't it?

John Yes.

Carol *Isn't* it ... ?

John Yes. I suppose.

Carol Now. The thing which you find so cruel is the selfsame process of selection I, and my group, go through *every day of our lives.* In admittance to school. In our tests, in our class rankings. ... Is it unfair? I can't tell you. But, if it is fair. Or even if it is 'unfortunate but necessary' for us, then, by God, so must it be for you. (*Pause.*) You write of your 'responsibility to the young.' Treat us with respect, and that will *show* you your responsibility. You write that education is just hazing. (*Pause.*) But we worked to get to this school. (*Pause.*) And some of us. (*Pause.*) Overcame prejudices. Economic, sexual, you cannot begin to imagine. And endured humiliations I *pray* that you and those you love never will encounter. (*Pause.*) To gain admittance here. To pursue that same dream of security *you* pursue. We, who, who are, at any moment, in danger of being deprived of it. By . . .

John   . . . by . . . ?

Carol   By the administration. By the teachers. By *you*. By, say, one low grade, that keeps us out of graduate school; by one, say, one capricious or inventive answer on our parts, which, perhaps, you don't find amusing. Now you *know*, do you see? What it is to be subject to that power. (*Pause.*)

John   I don't understand. (*Pause.*)

Carol   My charges are not trivial. You see that in the haste, I think, with which they were accepted. A *joke* you have told, with a sexist tinge. The language you use, a verbal or physical caress, yes, yes, I know, you say that it is meaningless. I understand. I differ from you. To lay a hand on someone's shoulder.

John   It was devoid of sexual content.

Carol   I say it was not. I SAY IT WAS NOT. Don't you begin to *see* . . . ? Don't you begin to understand? IT'S NOT FOR YOU TO SAY.

John   I take your point, and I see there is much good in what you refer to.

Carol   . . . do you think so . . . ?

John   . . . but, and this is not to say that I cannot change, in those things in which I am deficient . . . But, the . . .

Carol   Do you hold yourself harmless from the charge of sexual exploitativeness . . . ? (*Pause.*)

John   Well, I . . . I . . . I . . . You know I, as I said. I . . . think I am not too old to *learn*, and I *can* learn, I . . .

Carol   Do you hold yourself innocent of the charge of . . .

John   . . . wait, wait, wait . . . All right, let's go back to . . .

Carol   YOU FOOL. Who do you think I am? To come here and be taken in by a *smile*. You little yapping fool.

You think I want 'revenge.' I don't want revenge. I WANT UNDERSTANDING.

John   ... *do* you?

Carol   I do. (*Pause.*)

John   What's the use. It's over.

Carol   Is it? What is?

John   My job.

Carol   Oh. Your job. That's what you want to talk about. (*Pause.*) (*She starts to leave the room. She steps and turns back to him.*) All right. (*Pause.*) What if it were possible, that my Group withdraws its complaint. (*Pause.*)

John   What?

Carol   That's right. (*Pause.*)

John   Why.

Carol   Well, let's say as an act of friendship.

John   An act of friendship.

Carol   Yes. (*Pause.*)

John   In exchange for what.

Carol   Yes. But I don't think, 'exchange.' Not 'in exchange.' For what do we derive from it? (*Pause.*)

John   'Derive.'

Carol   Yes.

John   (*pause*) Nothing. (*Pause.*)

Carol   That's right. We derive nothing. (*Pause.*) Do you see that?

John   Yes.

Carol   That is a little word, Professor. 'Yes.' 'I see that.' But you will.

John   And you might speak to the committee ... ?

Carol   To the committee?

John   Yes.

Carol   Well. Of course. That's on your mind. We might.

John   'If ' what?

Carol   'Given' what. Perhaps. I think that that is more friendly.

John   GIVEN WHAT?

Carol   And, believe me, I understand your rage. It is not that I don't feel it. But I do not see that it is deserved, so I do not resent it. . . . All right. I have a list.

John   . . . a list.

Carol   Here is a list of books, which we . . .

John   . . . a list of books . . . ?

Carol   That's right. Which we find questionable.

John   What?

Carol   Is this so bizarre . . . ?

John   I can't believe . . .

Carol   It's not necessary you believe it.

John   Academic freedom . . .

Carol   Someone chooses the books. If you can choose them, others can. What are you, 'God'?

John   . . . no, no, the 'dangerous.' . . .

Carol   You have an agenda, we have an agenda. I am not interested in your feelings or your motivation, but your actions. If you would like me to speak to the Tenure Committee, here is my list. You are a Free Person, you decide. (*Pause.*)

John   Give me the list. (*She does so. He reads.*)

Carol   I think you'll find . . .

John   I'm capable of reading it. Thank you.

Carol   We have a number of *texts* we need re . . .

John   I see that.

Carol   We're amenable to . . .

John   Aha. Well, let me look over the . . . (*He reads.*)

Carol   I think that . . .

John   LOOK. I'm reading your demands. All right?! (*He reads.*) (*Pause.*) You want to ban my book?

Carol   We do not . . .

John (*of list*)   It says here . . .

Carol   . . . We want it removed from inclusion as a representative example of the university.

John   Get out of here.

Carol   If you put aside the issues of personalities.

John   Get the fuck out of my office.

Carol   No, I think I would reconsider.

John   . . . you think you can.

Carol   We can and we *will.* Do you want our support? That is the only quest . . .

John   . . . to ban my *book* . . . ?

Carol   . . . that is correct . . .

John   . . . this . . . this is a *university* . . . we . . .

Carol   . . . and we have a statement . . . which we need you to . . . (*She hands him a sheet of paper.*)

John   No, no. It's out of the question. I'm sorry. I don't know what I was thinking of. I want to tell you something. I'm a teacher. I am a teacher. Eh? It's my *name* on the door, and *I* teach the class, and that's what I do. I've got a book with my name on it. And my son will *see* that *book* someday. And I have a respon ... No, I'm sorry I have a *responsibility* ... to *myself*, to my son, to my *profession*. ... I haven't been *home* for two days, do you know that? Thinking this out.

Carol ... you haven't?

John I've been, no. If it's of interest to you. I've been in a *hotel. Thinking. (The phone starts ringing.) Thinking* ...

Carol ... you haven't been home?

John ... *thinking*, do you see.

Carol Oh.

John And, and, I owe you a debt, I see that now. (*Pause.*) You're *dangerous*, you're *wrong* and it's my *job* ... to say no to you. That's my job. You are absolutely right. You want to ban my book? Go to *hell*, and they can do whatever they want to me.

Carol ... you haven't been home in two days ...

John I think I told you that.

Carol ... you'd better get that phone. (*Pause.*) I think that you should pick up the phone. (*Pause.*)

John *picks up the phone.*

John (*on phone*) Yes. (*Pause.*) Yes. Wh ... I. I. I had to be away. All ri ... did they wor ... did they worry ab ... No. I'm all right, now, Jerry. I'm f ... I got a little turned *around*, but I'm *sitting* here and ... I've got it figured out. I'm fine. I'm fine don't worry about me. I got a little bit mixed up. But I am not sure that it's not a blessing. It cost me my job? Fine. Then the job was not worth having. Tell Grace that I'm coming home and everything is fff ... (*Pause.*) What? (*Pause.*) *What? (Pause.)* What do you *mean?* WHAT? Jerry ... Jerry. They ... Who, who, what can they do ... ? (*Pause.*) NO. (*Pause.*) NO. They can't do th ... What do you mean? (*Pause.*) But how ... (*Pause.*) She's, she's, she's *here* with me. To ... Jerry. I don't underst ... (*Pause.*) (*He hangs up.*) (*To* **Carol**.) What does this mean?

Carol I thought you knew.

John What. (*Pause.*) What does it mean. (*Pause.*)

Carol You tried to rape me. (*Pause.*) According to the law. (*Pause.*)

John ... what...?

Carol You tried to rape me. I was leaving this office, you 'pressed' yourself into me. You 'pressed' your body into me.

John ... I ...

Carol My Group has told your lawyer that we may pursue criminal charges.

John ... no ...

Carol ... under the statute. I am told. It was battery.

John ... no ...

Carol Yes. And attempted rape. That's right. (*Pause.*)

John I think that you should go.

Carol Of course. I thought you knew.

John I have to talk to my lawyer.

Carol Yes. Perhaps you should.

The phone rings again. Pause.

John (*picks up phone. Into phone*) Hello? I ... Hello ...? I ... Yes, he just called. No ... I. I can't talk to you now, Baby. (*To* **Carol**.) Get out.

Carol ... your wife ...?

John ... who it is is no concern of yours. Get out. (*To phone.*) No, no, it's going to be all right. I. I can't talk now, Baby. (*To* **Carol**.) Get out of here.

Carol I'm going.

John Good.

Carol (*exiting*) ... and don't call your wife 'baby.'

John　What?

Carol　Don't call your wife baby. You heard what I said.

Carol *starts to leave the room.* **John** *grabs her and begins to beat her.*

John　You vicious little bitch. You think you can come in here with your political correctness and destroy my life?

He knocks her to the floor.

After how I treated you . . . ? You should be . . . *Rape you* . . . ? Are you kidding me . . . ?

He picks up a chair, raises it above his head, and advances on her.

I wouldn't touch you with a ten-foot pole. You little *cunt* . . .

She cowers on the floor below him. Pause. He looks down at her. He lowers the chair. He moves to his desk, and arranges the papers on it. Pause. He looks over at her.

. . . well . . .

Pause. She looks at him.

Carol　Yes. That's right.

She looks away from him, and lowers her head. To herself.

. . . yes. That's right.

The Cryptogram

This play is dedicated to Gregory Mosher

The Cryptogram was first performed in the United States at the American Repertory Theatre, Massachusetts, on 2 February 1995.

The Cryptogram was first performed in the United Kingdom at the Ambassadors Theatre, London, on 29 June 1994. The cast was as follows:

Donny	Lindsay Duncan
Del	Eddie Izzard
John	Danny Worters/Richard Claxton

Directed by Gregory Mosher
Designed by Bob Crowley
Lighting by Rick Fisher

Act One

A living room. One door leading off to the kitchen.
One staircase leading up to the second floor.

Evening. **Del** *is seated on the couch.* **John** *comes downstairs dressed in his pajamas.*

John I couldn't find 'em.

Del . . . couldn't find 'em.

John No.

Del What?

John Slippers.

Del Mmm?

John Packed.

Del . . . slippers are packed.

John Yes.

Del Why did you pack them?

John Take them along.

Del How are you going to use your slippers up there?

John To keep my feet warm.

Del Mmm.

John I shouldn't of packed them?

Del Well, put something on your feet.

John What?

Del Socks.

John Put something on my feet now.

Del Yes.

John   'As long as I'm warm.'

Del   That's correct.

John   I have 'em. (*Produces socks. Starts putting them on.*)

Del   That's good. Think ahead.

John   Why did you say 'why did you pack them?'?

Del   I wondered that you'd take them with.

John   Why?

Del   Out in the Woods?

John   No, but to wear in the Cabin.

Del   . . . that's right.

John   Don't you think?

Del   I do.

John   I know I couldn't wear them in the woods.

Del   No. No. That's right. Where were we?

John   Issues of sleep.

Del   . . . iss . . . ?

John   Issues of sleep.

Del   No. I'm sorry. You were quite correct. To take your slippers. I spoke too quickly.

John   That's alright.

Del   Thank you. (*Pause.*) Where were we? Issues of Sleep.

John   And last night either.

Del   Mm . . . ?

John   . . . I couldn't sleep.

Del   So I'm told. (*Pause.*)

John   Last night, either.

Del   Fine. What does it mean 'I could not sleep'?

John . . . what does it mean?

Del Yes. It means nothing other than the meaning you choose to assign to it.

John I don't get you.

Del I'm going to explain myself.

John Good.

Del A 'Trip', for example, you've been looking forward to.

John A trip. Yes. Oh, yes.

Del . . . absolutely right.

John . . . that I'm excited.

Del . . . who wouldn't be?

John *Anyone* would be.

Del That's right.

John . . . to go in the Woods . . . ?

Del Well. You see? You've answered your own question. (*Pause.*)

John Yes. I'm excited.

Del I can't blame you.

John You can't.

Del No. Do you see?

John That it's natural.

Del I think it is.

John Is it?

Del I think it absolutely is. To go with your father . . . ?

John Why isn't he home?

Del We don't know.

John ... because it's something. To go out there.

Del I should say.

John In the Woods ... ?

Del I hope to tell you.

John Well, you *know* it is.

Del That I do. And I will tell you: older people, too. Grown people. You know what they do? The night before a trip?

John What do they do?

Del Well, many times *they* cannot sleep. *They* will stay up that night.

John They will?

Del Oh yes.

John Why?

Del They can't sleep. No. Why? Because their minds, you see, are full of thoughts.

John What are their thoughts of?

Del Their thoughts are of two things.

John Yes?

Del Of what they're *leaving*.

John ... yes?

Del And what they're going *toward*. (*Pause.*) Just like you.

John ... of what they're leaving ...

Del ... mmm ... (*Pause.*)

John How do you know that ...

A crash is heard offstage.

Donny (*offstage*) ... I'm alright ...

Del ... what?

Donny (*offstage*) I'm alright . . .

Del . . . did . . .

Donny (*offstage*) What? Did I what?

Del Are you . . .

Donny (*offstage*) What? I've spilt the tea.

Del What?

Donny (*offstage*) I spilled the tea.

Del Do you want help?

Donny (*offstage*) What?

John 'Do you want help' he said.

Donny (*offstage*) No.

Del You don't? (*To* **John**.) Go help your mother . . .

Donny (*offstage*) . . . I'm alright. (*To self.*) Oh, hell . . .

Del What did you . . .

Donny (*offstage*) What?

Del . . . what did . . .

Donny I broke the tea, I broke the teapot. I'm alright. I broke the teapot. (*Pause.*)

Del (*to* **John**) Well there you go.
. . . a human *being* . . .

John . . . yes?

Del . . . cannot conceal himself.

John That's an example?

Del Well, hell, look at it: anything. When it is *disordered*, any um, 'change' do you see . . . ?

John She ain't going.

Del No of course she's not. But *you* are. And your father is. It's an upheaval.

John   It's a minor one

Del   Who is to say?

John   But did *you* feel that?

Del   Did I . . . ?

John   Yes.

Del · Feel what?

John   Last week.

Del   Feel. Last week.

John   Thoughts on a trip. When you took *your* trip.

Donny (*off*)   It's going to be a minute . . .

John   . . . when you . . .

Donny (*off*)   . . . hello . . . ?

Del   We're alright.

Donny (*off*)   The tea is going to be a minute.

John   We're alright in here.

Donny (*entering*)   I've put the . . . why aren't you asleep.

Del   . . . did I feel 'pressure'?

Donny   . . . John? . . .

John   Yes.

Donny   Why aren't you asleep?

Del   Before my trip. No.

John   No. Why?

Del   Because, and this is important. Because people differ.

Donny   What are you doing down here?

Del   We're talking.

John   . . . I came down.

Del (*to* **Donny**) I'm sorry. Are you alright?

Donny What? I dropped the teapot.
What are you *doing* down . . .

John We're talking.

Del He came down, and I began a conversation.

Donny (*sighs*) We're going to have tea, and then you go
upst – Where are your slippers?

John Packed.

Donny They're packed.

John For the trip.

Donny And then you go upstairs and you go to sleep.

John I want to wait 'til he comes home.

Donny Well, yes, I'm sure you do. But you need your
sleep. And if you don't get it, you're not . . .

John Will he be home soon?

Donny Yes. He will.

John Where is he?

Donny I don't know. Yes, I do, yes. He's at the Office.
And he'll be home soon.

John Why is he working late?

Donny I don't know. We'll find out when he comes
home, John. Must we do this ev –

John I only want . . .

Donny Do you know what? I think that it is important
that you . . .

John I didn't want to upset you.

Del (*simultaneous with 'upset'*) Could I make a suggestion?
(*To* **John**.) Why don't you busy yourself?

Donny He has to sleep.

Del ... but he's not going to sleep. He's ...

John That's right.

Donny (*simultaneous with 'He's'*) No. You're absolutely right.

John ... something to do. If I had *that* ...

Del Are you packed?

John I'm all packed.

Del ... well ...

John I, I, My *Father* isn't packed. His ...

Donny No. No, I'll tell you what you could do.

John What?

Donny Close the attic up.

John ... close it up?

Donny Neaten it up. Yes.

John Is it disturbed?

Donny ... after my 'rummaging'.

John Alright.

Donny ... and ...

John ... alright.

Donny See if you find any things up there.

John Things.

Donny ... you might need to take.

John ... things I might need to take up.

Donny Mm.

John Or that *he* might need.

Donny That's right.

John ... or that you forgot.

Donny   Yes.

John   To pack.

Donny   Yes. Would you do that?

John   Of course.

Donny   Thank you, John.

Del   Thank you.

Donny   And perhaps you'd put on some clothing.

John   Good.

Donny   Very good. Off you go then.

John   I will.

Del   'My blessings on your House'.

John   'And mine on yours.'

Del   'Until the whale shall speak.'

John   'Until the Moon shall Weep.'

Del   'Until we need no further . . .'

John (*exiting*)   I will, good. (*Pause.*)

Donny   No. I don't understand it.

Del   Well . . .

Donny   No.

Del   He has trouble sleeping.

Donny   Mm. No.

Del   That's his nature.

Donny   Is it?

Del   Children . . .

Donny   No. You see. It's grown into this rodomontade. Every night . . .

Del   Well, yes. But this is *special*, he . . .

Donny   No, No. He always has a reason. Some ... every night ...

Del   Yes. Granted. But a Trip to the Woods ...

Donny   ... he ...

Del   ... with his Dad ...? It's an *event*. I think. What do I know? But, as his *friend* ...

Donny   Yes. Yes. He Always has a Reason.

Del   Yes, but I'm saying, in *spite* of ... I don't know. I don't mean to intrude ... but good. But *Good*. One sends him up to the Attic ...

Donny   Oh. Oh oh ...

Del   To, um ... to, um, what is the word ...?

Donny   Look what I found.

Del   To um ...

Donny   Del. Shut up.

Del   'Participate.' That's the word.

Donny   Look what I found in the attic.

She goes to a sidetable and brings back a small framed photograph and hands it to **Del**.

Del (*pause*)   When was this ...?

Donny   When I was packed for the ... Isn't it ...

Del   No, no. When was this taken?

Donny   Isn't it funny? Though? (*Pause.*) The things that you find? (*Pause.*)

Del   I don't understand this picture. (*Pause.*)

Donny   What do you mean?

John *comes down onto the landing.*

John   Which coat? That's what I forgot. To pack my ...

Donny (*to* **Del**) Which coat?

Del What?

Donny Which . . .

John That's what was on my mind.

Donny Which coat should he take?

Del (*looking up from the photograph*) When were you up there?

Donny Mm?

Del Up in the attic?

Donny (*simultaneous with 'attic'*) Today.

Del (*of photo*) . . . this is the damnedest thing . . .

Donny *Isn't* it . . . ? And I found that old *Lap* robe.

Del The lap robe . . .

Donny The *stadium* blanket we . . .

John Which coat?

Donny Which?

John How cold is it up there yet?

Del . . . a lap robe . . .

John How cold was it last week? Del?

Donny Just bring your regular coat.

John My blue coat?

Donny The melton coat?

John What's melton?

Donny The blue coat. Your fabric coat.

John The *wool* one?

Donny (*to* **Del**) Is it too cold for that?

Del No.

Donny   Then take it.

John   My *blue* coat.

Donny   Yes.

John   Do I have any sweaters left?

Donny   Up there?

John   Yes.

Del   I think so.

Donny   I'm sure that you do.

John   You think so?

Del   They'd be in your bureau.

John   And, the fishing stuff. Is it there?

Donny   The fishing stuff. They brought back. Last week. It's all . . .

John   . . . they brought it back.

Donny   Yes. It's up in the attic . . .

John (*simultaneous with 'attic'*)   You should have left it at the Cabin.

Donny   It's in the back. You'll see it up there.

Del   . . . we were afraid . . .

Donny   . . . they didn't want it to get stolen.

John   And the fishing line. Do we have that good . . .

Del   . . . we were afraid it would get taken.

John   . . . that good line . . . ?

Donny   . . . I'm sorry, John . . . ?

John   The fishing line.

Donny   I'm sure you. Yes. Fishing line. In the same box.

John   Green? The green one?

Donny   ... I ...

John   The green line. Because if not, we have to stop on the way, and ...

Donny   ... I'm ...

John   Dad said that the green line ...

Del   What's special about it?

Donny   Open the box.

John   ... because if not ...

Donny   Find the box. Open it, and check it out.

John   Well, because, that's how we'll know. (*Exits, up the stairs.*)

Donny   And put some clothing on. (*Pause.*)

Del (*of photo*)   ... when was this taken?

Donny   I swear. He's ...

Del   What? Well, he's having difficulty sleeping.

Donny   It's all such a mystery.

Del   Do you think?

Donny   All our good intentions ...

Del   Big thing. Going in the Woods. Your Father ...

Donny   ... mmm.

Del   ... big thing.

Donny (*pause*)   It goes so quickly.

Del   Certain things remain. (*Pause.*) Friendship ... (*Pause.*)

Donny (*to herself*)   It goes so quickly ... Sometimes I wish I was a monk.

Del   Like in the book?

Donny   And just *sit.*

Del   Well that's a, you know, that's a form of
meditation . . .

John   *re-enters, wrapped in a plaid blanket.*

Donny   No. That's not clothing.

John   . . . I . . .

Donny   You put some clothing on right now. (*Pause.*)
What? (*Pause.*)

John   I tore it.

Donny   You tore what?

John   I tore the blanket. I'm sorry.

Donny   You tore it?

John   (*simultaneous with 'tore'*)   I was opening the box. I
think that there was a nail. I heard something rip . . .

He shows the tear.

Donny   You tore *that* blanket?

John   I heard some . . .

Donny   (*simultaneous with 'some'*)   John, that was done so
long ago.

John   I heard it rip.

Donny   No. It was torn so long ago.

John   (*simultaneous with 'ago'*)   I didn't tear it?

Donny   No.

John   I heard it rip.

Del   You may have heard it in your mind . . .

John   . . . but . . .

Donny   No, we tore that long ago.

Del   I think your mind is racing.

Donny   It's alright, John. It's alright. Go upstairs. And you put some clothing . . .

John It's tied with twine.

Donny I don't understand you.

John The *box* . . .

Donny Box . . . ?

John . . . with the fishing . . .

Donny Well, *untie* it. And . . .

John I can't untie it. That's what I'm saying. I tried to pull the twine off, but . . .

Del (*takes out knife. Of knife*) . . . is it alright . . . ?

Donny . . . If you don't get some rest before . . .

Del (*to* **Donny**) Is it alright?

Donny (*to* **Del**) What? (*To* **John**. *Of knife.*) What would your father say?

John It's alright.

Donny It's alright for you to have the knife . . . ?

John Yes.

Donny . . . it's alr –

John Where did you get the knife . . . ?

Donny Good *Lord*, John . . . calm *down* tonight.

John No.

Donny . . . why not?

John The Tea, the Blanket . . . ?

Donny I don't understand.

John I'm *waiting* for it.

Del You're waiting for what?

John 'The Third . . .'

Del   'The Third Misfortune.'

Donny   Third . . . ?

John   'What is the Third Misfortune?'

Donny   . . . who . . . ?

John   It's in the book.

Donny   Where *is* that book . . .

Del   Misfortunes come in threes.

Donny   (*simultaneous with 'threes'*) The Third Misfortune.
Yes.

John   . . . it's in the book.

Donny   . . . and you've remembered it all this . . .

John   'Far from the press of information, *knowledge* . . .'

Del   'When we think of Sickness, sickness is
approaching . . .'

Donny   And misfortunes come in th . . . (*To* **Del**.) Where
is that Book?

Del   It will turn up someday.

Donny   And what were the others?

John   The Lance, and the Chalice: the . . .

Donny   No. Here.

John   What are the others here?

Donny   The Three Misfortunes.

John   One: The Teapot broke.

Donny   That's one, yes. And?

John   The blank . . .

Del   . . . the blanket.

Donny   What about it?

John   . . . torn . . .

Donny   No, but it *wasn't* torn. That happened long ago.

John   I *thought* I tore it now.

Sound of kettle, **Donny** *exits.*

Donny   It was torn long ago. You can absolve your . . .

John   . . . I *thought* that I tore it.

Del   But, you see, in reality, things unfold . . .

John *hands the knife back to* **Del.**

. . . thank you . . . independent of our fears of them.

John   I don't know what you mean.

Del   Because we *think* a thing is one way does not mean that this is the way that this thing must be.

John   . . . it was torn long ago?

Del   That's what your mother said.

John   How? Did you see my hat?

Del   . . . did?

John   At the Cabin?

Del   Which hat is that?

John   The grey cap.

Del   Like mine except grey?

John   Yes.

Del   I don't remember.

John   Not like yours. Actually it's . . .

Del   I don't remember.

John   No, it's not actually like yours, it's . . .

Del   How is it different?

John   It's – I steered you wrong. It's not like yours at all.

Del   Then I don't know which one you mean.

John   My *grey* hat. It was on the peg.

Del   I don't remember.

John   You don't? Why?

Del   Because I wasn't looking for it.

John   . . . I . . .

Del   Do you want to know . . . I'm going to tell you a game.

John   A game?

Del   A game you can play.
You and your father. Up there. Eh?
To 'sharpen your skills'. (*Pause.*) To 'aid your camping'.

John   Me and my father.

Del   Yes.

John   Does he know this game?

Del   I think that he may.

John   Did he teach it to you?

Del   No. I learned it independently.

John   Um.

Del   And. If he does not know it, you can teach it to *him*.

John   Good.

Del   Yes? You think so?

John   Well, I think so. You have to tell me the game.

Del   Here it is: . . . you write down . . .

John   '. . . to sharpen our skills . . .'

Del   You write down your *recollections*. Of the things you've seen. During the day. Then you compare them.

John   I don't understand.

Del To see who has observed the best. You observe things during the day. Then at night you write them down. To test your observation. (*Pause.*) Things in the Cabin for instance. Or the woods. And then you see whose recollection was more accurate. (*Pause.*) You see?

John See who was more accurate.

Del That's right. (*Pause.*)

John And why is this game useful?

Del If you were lost it could assist you to orient yourself.

John Would it be things which we *decided before* to observe? Or things . . .

Del . . . it could be both.

John . . . both things we *decided* to observe, and things we decided, later on, we should remember.

Del That's right.

John But something could have been the 'Third Misfortune' even though it had happened quite long ago. (*Pause.*)

Del How could that be?

John It could be if the 'Third Misfortune' happened long ago. If, when it *happened*, no one *noticed*, or . . .

Del 'at the time . . .'

John Yes, or neglected to *count* it . . .

Del . . . I . . .

John . . . until we recognized it now . . . And also, what could we pick. To observe, beside the Cabin?

Del What? *Anything.* The *pond*, the . . .

John . . . where did you get the knife?

Del The knife.

John That's right.

Del   Your father gave it to me.

John   He gave you his knife.

Del   Yes.

John   His *war* knife . . . ?

Del   Yes. (*Pause.*)

John   But we couldn't choose the pond.

Del   Why not?

John   Because it's changing. (*Pause.*) When?

Del   . . . when what?

John   Did he give it to you?

Del   Aha.

John   When?

Del   Last week.

John   When you went up?

Del   Does it upset you?

John   No.

Del   Aha.

John   What do you mean?

Del   Aha.

John   We couldn't choose the pond.

Donny *re-enters with tea tray.*
Del *clears coffee table, picks up photo.*

Del   Well, then you just choose something else.

John   What should I choose?

Del   Something that doesn't change. (*Of photo.*) Who, who, what *is* this?

Donny   It's the Lake.

Del   No please I know where it is, I just don't . . .

Donny   . . . what?

Del   . . . I don't remember it.

John (*of photo*)   You have a strange expression on your face. *Mother:* doesn't . . .

Donny   Calm down. John.

Del   . . . I do?

John   You're grinning. (*To* **Donny**.) I am calm.

Del   . . . when was this taken? (**Donny** *looks at photograph*.)

Donny   Well, the boathouse is still up . . .

Del (*to* **John**)   It's strange I'm grinning?

Donny   . . . so it's . . .

John   It looks unlike you.

Donny (*of photograph. To* **Del**)   You don't remember this?

Del   No.

Donny   We're . . .

Del   . . . the boathouse is up, but the *birch* is down, so . . . I can tell you what *year* it is: the boathouse is up, but the birch is down, so: it's before the War . . . (**John** *yawns, sits on the couch*.)

Donny   Oh John; are you getting sleepy?

John   When is Dad coming home?

Donny   He'll be here when he gets here. I think.

John   . . . I want to tell him this game.

Del (*of photograph*)   I remember the shirt.

Donny   . . . he'll be home soon, John.

Del   . . . is this Robert's shirt?

Donny   That *you're* wearing?

Del Yes . . .

Donny . . . I . . . (*Pause.*)

Del He's asleep.

Donny *Finally.* (*Pause.*) He thought that he tore the blanket.

Del I believe that this Trip has a 'meaning' for him.

Donny Del, he's always had this problem.

Del No, because, I've had a 'clue'.

Donny No, Robert always said: we disagreed about it. From the first. And his theory was 'let him cry'.

Del No, this trip . . .

Donny He Always Has a Reason . . .

Del He's a 'sensitive kid' . . . ?

Donny . . . whatever that means.

Del I think it means . . . Well, I didn't know what it means, but he *told* me, in effect.

Donny . . . yes?

Del That in this case it means he's *jealous*.

Donny Jealous.

Del Of my trip. Last week with Robert.

Donny He was jealous?

Del That's right.

Donny But why does that come out *now*?
And I'll tell you one other thing.
Let him be jealous. What if he was? Yes. I think he has to spend more time with his father; and, yes, I think that he has to learn the world does not revolve around him.
(*Pause.*)
Oh, Lord, I'll tell you. No. You're right. It's *guilt*.
I get to spend a weekend on my own.

Del (*of photograph*)   Who took this picture?

Pause. **Donny** *looks at it.*

Donny   I don't know.

Del   Eh? Who could have taken it?

Donny   Huh. (*Pause.*) I don't . . .

Del   Do you see? If we're all in it? (*Pause.*) That's why I don't remember it.

Donny   I . . . (*Pause.*) Isn't that funny . . . ?

Del   That's why I don't remember it.

Donny   Lord, I found so much *stuff* up there.

Del   . . . up . . . ?

Donny   In the attic. The *stadium* blanket . . . , the –

Del   I recognized that.

Donny   How could he think he tore it? He's seen it for years.

Del   Mm.

Donny   . . . so long ago . . .

Del (*simultaneous with 'ago'*)   Do you know, at the Hotel. I collect things. I'm amazed. I clean my room out. Every few months. I'm amazed. I always think I've kept it *bare*. But when I clean it out. I find this mass of *things* I have accumulated.

Donny   They, what are they, mostly?

Del   Papers.

Donny   I went to the Point.

Del   You did?

Donny   I walked down there. (*Pause.*) Yes.

Del   When? Recently?

Donny Yes. (*Pause.*)
And I remembered. When the three of us would go. Late at night. Summers.

Del I remember.

Donny *Robert* and I . . . (*Pause.*) And we were making love. Under the blanket. And I wondered. After all this time, why it never occurred to me. To wonder. Did you *hear* us; and, if you did. If it upset you. (*Pause.*)

Del And you've thought about it all this time. (*Pause.*) Oh Donny.

Donny Did it upset you?

Del You sweet thing.

Donny Did it?

Del Well I . . .

John (*waking*) What did they say? What?

Donny Go to sleep, John.

John I was going there. But you said to bring the, bring . . . (*Pause.*) Bring them the . . . (*Pause.*)

Donny John:

John . . . huh . . .

Donny It's alright.

John What did they talk about?

Donny John . . .

John I . . . What? Is my father back yet?

Donny No. Why don't you go and get in bed . . .

John When is he coming back?

Donny Very soon, I think.

John He is?

Donny Yes. Is that alright?

John (*of photograph*)   You asked if the shirt you're wearing is his shirt.

Del   What?

John   . . . in . . .

Del   The photograph.

John   In the photograph.

Del   Is that His Shirt. Yes.

John   Well: does it *look* like his shirt?

Del   It's hard to tell. The picture is old . . .

John (*to* **Donny**)   I didn't tear the blanket?

Donny   No.

John   You're certain.

Donny   We've had it for years.

John   I don't remember it.

Donny   Yes. You would. If you thought about it.

John   What was it?

Donny   What? Go to sleep.

John   What did you use it for?

Donny   What did I use it for? A coverlet.

John   To keep you warm.

Donny   That's right.

John   A coverlet.

Donny   That's right.

John   Where did it come from?

Donny   Where? In England.

John   England.

Donny   Yes. From an Arcade.

John   Arcade . . .

Donny   With stores on either side.

John   Did you buy it together?

Donny   No. I bought it when he was away.

John   Away.

Donny   Yes. One day.

John   Away in the War.

Donny   That's right. (*Pause.*)

John   Did you miss him when he was gone?

Donny   Yes I did.

John   What did you think about? (*Pause.*)

Donny   Many things.

John   What things did you think of?

Donny   I don't know. *Many* things.

John   Were you frightened for him?

Donny   Yes. I was.

John   Did you tell him?

Donny   We used to go out. To the Country, you know . . .

John   Is it wool . . . ?

Donny   When he was back . . . walk in a *field*, or . . .

John   Is it wool?

Donny   I'm sorry?

John   Is it wool.

Donny   You know. When you were small. *You* slept in it. All of the time. We covered you. We . . .

John   Why did you stop using it.

Donny We put it away.

John Why?

Donny It was torn. (*Pause.*) And now you go to sleep.

John Do you ever think you hear singing?

Donny I don't know what you mean.

John *Singing.*

Donny I don't know, John I . . .

John At night. When you are asleep. Before you go to sleep.

Donny I don't know.

John . . . and you hear . . .

Donny . . . it's time for bed, now . . .

John . . . or you think you hear a radio . . .

Donny . . . I don't know . . .

John Playing *music.* And you think: 'Yes, I know. That's a radio.' And you listen. But then, you say: 'It's just in my head.' But you can *listen* to it. It goes on. Or *water* running. (*Pause.*) Or *voices.*

Donny You hear voices?

John Just before you go to sleep. Do you ever do that? (*Pause.*) I hear them. Outside my room.

Donny What are they saying?

John Do you ever do that?

Donny I don't know.

Del What are your voices saying?

John (*simultaneous with 'saying'*) Tell me how the blanket was torn.

Donny You go to sleep now, John.

John   It's time to go to sleep.

Donny   That's right.

John   Is that right?

Donny   You have a big . . .

John   *Tomorrow.*

Donny   Yes.

John   I'm going to do that thing.

Donny   What thing is that?

John   The game.

Donny   . . . the game.

John   To remember. The game. With my father.

Donny   The game. Yes.

John *starts upstairs.*

Donny   You take the blanket.

John   . . . but it would have to be some thing that would surprise us.

Donny   That's right.

John   When we look around.

He continues up the stairs. Stops to lean over the landing. Looking down at the mantelpiece.

So, I'll ask my Dad. First thing. 'You tell me the name of an *object*.' Or a '*collection* of things' . . . you know what I mean. '*A view* . . .'

Del   . . . that's right.

John   'As we approach the Cabin.'

Del   That's right.

John   But it doesn't have to be the Cabin.

Del   No . . .

John   It could be anywhere . . .

Del   That's right.

John   It could be anywhere at all.

Del   That's right. As long as it's some *thing*. You have determined to observe.

John   Yes. It could be right here . . .

Donny (*goes to him with the blanket, simultaneous with 'and'*)   . . . and take the blanket . . .

John *picks up white envelope on the mantelpiece.*

Donny (*of envelope*)   What's that?

John   It's a note . . . There's a note for you.

Donny *takes it, opens it.*

John   And it could be something right here, anything that, that, it would have to be something new . . . something that would

Donny (*reading*)   . . . that's right . . .

John   . . . *surprise* us.

Donny   . . . when did this get here . . . ?

John   . . . you see?

Donny   John. Go to bed. Now. Yes.

John   Do you see?

Donny   Go to bed.

John   Alright. I understand. I'm going. (**John** *exits.*)

Del   What is it?

Donny   It's a letter. (*Pause.*)

Del   What does it say? (*Pause.*)

Donny   Robert's leaving me.

Del   He's leaving you. (*Pause.*) Why would he want to do that?

Act Two

The next night.

John, *in his bathrobe, and* **Donny**.

John I thought that maybe there was nothing there. (*Pause.*) I thought that nothing was *there*. Then I was looking at my *book*. I thought 'Maybe there's nothing *in* my book.' It talked about the *buildings*. Maybe there's nothing *in* the buildings. And ... or on my *globe*. You know my globe? You know my globe?

Donny Yes.

John Maybe there's nothing on the thing that it is of. We don't know what's there. *We* don't know that those things are there.

Donny I've been there. To many of them.

John Or in *buildings* we have not been in. Or in *history*. In the *history* of things. Or *thought*. (*Pause.*) I was *lying* there, and maybe there is no such thing as *thought*. Who *says* there is? Or human beings. And we are a dream. Who knows we are here? No one knows we are. We are a dream. We are just *dreaming*. I *know* we are. Or else ... or else ... (*Pause.*) ... and how do we *know* the things we know? We don't know what's real. And all we do is *say* things. (*Pause.*) Where do we *get* them from? And, or that things, go on forever. (*Pause.*) Or that we're *born*. Or that dead people moan. Or that, or that there's *hell*. And maybe they are there. Maybe there are people who've *been* there. Or, or else why should we *think* it? That's what I don't know. And maybe *everything* is true. Maybe it's true that I'm *sitting* here ...

Donny Johnnie.

John What ... ?

Donny I think ...

John . . . don't you think?

Donny . . . you have to . . .

John No. I don't.

Donny Please, please do, though.

John I don't want to, though.

Del *enters.*

John (*of* **Del**) That's what I mean. I don't want to.
Mother . . . didn't you, Mother. Mother . . .

Donny (*to* **Del**) Did you . . .

Del (*simultaneous with* 'you') No.

Donny Did you find him?

Del (*to* **John**) How are you? (*To* **Donny**.) No.

John I'm fine.

Donny Where did you . . .

Del The *Windermere*, and then I stopped at Jimmy's.

Donny Did you try the Eagle?

Del No. (*Unpacking his paper bag.*) How has he . . .

Donny Why *not*? Why *not*?

Del I'm sorry . . . why not what?

Donny (*simultaneous with* 'what') Why didn't you go to
the . . .

Del . . . I thought you were going to call th . . .

Donny Why should I call them, if they'll say he wasn't
there? Even if he *is* there . . . ?

Del (*simultaneous with* 'there') I thought you were going to
call them.

Donny (*simultaneous with* 'call') No. I never said that.

Del Well, then. I made a mistake. (*He is preparing syrup* *from medicine bottle, several other bottles stand around.*)

Donny   How much was it?

Del   I told them to charge it to you.
(*Holding spoon. To* **John**.) Open your mouth.

John   I don't want to take that stuff.

Donny   You're going to take it and you're going to *sleep*.

John   No. I'm not sleepy.

Donny   Take the medicine. Did you *hear* me? You're *sick*, and you're going to *bed*.

John   I can't *sleep*.

Del   . . . that's why . . .

John   Every time I go to sleep I *see* things . . .

Donny   You must . . .

Del   That's, that's why you have to take the medicine, John.

John (*simultaneous with 'John'*)   No. I'm not tired.

Donny   Do you want to go to the Hospital?

John   No.

Donny   No? Did you hear what the Doctor said?

John   No.

Del   . . . what did he say?

Donny   I want you to go to bed *now*.

Del   You heard your . . .

John   No. No.

Donny   Johnnie . . .

John   No one understands. You think that I'm *in* something . . . You don't know what I'm feeling.

Del   What are you feeling? (*Pause.*) Are you afraid to go to bed?

John   Yes.

Donny   Why?

Del   What are you afraid of in there?

John   I don't know.

Donny   I . . . I . . . I know it *frightens* you . . .

John   I don't want to go to sleep.

Del   Alright, alright. I'm going to *promise* you . . . look at me. John. I'm going to *promise* you if you take this and . . . you take this and go upstairs then you won't be afraid. I promise. (*Pause.*) I promise you. (*Pause.*)

John   I sweat through the sheets . . .

Del   We'll change . . .

John   . . . the *bed* is wet.

Del   We'll change, we'll change the sheets, you don't have to . . .

Donny   You go lie down in my bed.

Del   . . . you lie down in your mother's bed. (*Pause.*) You go lie down there.

John   I'm going to sweat them.

Del   That's alright. Do you hear what I'm telling you . . . ?

John   Maybe I'll just . . . maybe I'll just go there . . . maybe I'll just go there and lie down.

Donny   Yes. You go and lie down now. You take this, now.

Del *gives* **John** *his medicine.*

John   Do you know why I took it, cause I'm tired.

Del   I'm sure you are.

John   . . . cause I've been *up* all day . . .

Del   I know you have. And I know how that feels.

John   I ... I ...

Donny   ... you go to bed now.

Del   John? 'My blessings on this house' ...

Pause. **John** *starts to cry.*

John   When is my father coming for me ... ?

Donny   Shhhh.

John   ... No. I don't understand.

Donny   Shh. It's alright.

John   What's happening to me ... ?

Donny (*embracing him*)   It's alright. Hush. You go to bed. It's alright. John. Shh. You've only got a fever. Shhh ...

Del   ... you're fine ...

Donny   You go upstairs now. Shhh. You go upstairs now, John ... (*She starts him upstairs. Comes down.*)

Del   ... I looked every place I thought that he would be ...

Donny   I'm sorry.

Del   Do you want a drink?

Donny   No. (*Pause.*)

Del   I'm sorry that I couldn't find him. Would you like me to go out again?

Donny   No. (*Pause.*)

Del   Would you like to play Casino?

Donny   No.

Del   Would you like to play Gin? Oh, God, oh God, that's *stupid.* (*Pause.*) That's, that's, that's, that's ... (*Pause.*) Do you see what I mean when I talk about myself? (*Pause.*) But would you like to?

Donny   Let's have a drink.

Del   Well. I know I'm limited.

Del *goes to the liquor cabinet, examines bottles.*

There's only a new one.

Donny   That's alright, open it.

He takes out bottle, takes out his knife, opens bottle.

Del   Enough. Enough for one day. I don't care. I think that this is good for you. (*Pause.*) You know why. . . . ? Because it's a ceremony. To, to *delimit* umm

Donny   A ceremony.

Del   Of . . . of what? Of, of *inebriation*, certainly, of, of of well, of *togetherness* . . . I don't know.

He goes to the kitchen, comes out with two glasses and the bottle. Pours two glasses.

Donny   Thank you.

Del   Uh . . . Days May Come, Days May Go . . . (*Long pause.*) Well, *that's* true enough . . .

Donny   Ha.

Del   Uhhhh . . .

Donny   May We Always be as . . .

Del   Yes.

Donny   As . . .

Del   Unified . . .

Donny   Well, let's pick something more moving than that.

Del   Alright . . . be.be.be.be.be-*nighted*? No, that's not the word I want to use . . . be-*trothed* . . . ? No.

Donny   Close . . .

Del   Yes.

Donny Close to each other.

Del As we happen to be right now. (*Pause.*)

Donny Oh, Lord ...

They clink glasses and drink.

Del Have another drink. (*He pours.*) Um ... um ... um ... (*Pause.*) And ... May the Spirit of Friendship ... oh, the hell with it. I mean, can't two people just have a drink ... for the love of God?

Donny Oh, Lord ...

Del Bec ... because I swear, because I think there's just too much. In trial ... in adversity ... (*Pause.*) and you can't, you can't go always look ...

Donny Go looking for answers ...

Del No.

Donny ... you're absolutely right ...

Del In intro*spec*tion.

Donny No.

Del ... at times of *trial* ...

Donny ... no.

Del Do you hear what I'm telling you?

Donny Yes.

Del ... they come for us all.

Donny ... Oh, Lord.

Del Yes. They do. Many times the answer comes. In reaching out. How can I watch you suffer? Or, do you know what? In getting drunk.

Donny ... in drinking.

Del Be ... Because, you know? Then you forget. (*Pause.*) And I don't *give* a damn. (*Pause.*) In this *shithole*. (*Pause.*)

Where friends . . . Well. I'm not going to *dwell* upon it.
(*Pause.*) You drink. And then, when you *remember* again . . .
(*Pause.*) It's later on. And time has dulled your, your . . .
you know, for whatever portion of time that, that you
forgot. (*Pause.*)

Donny 'You should get married.'

Del 'It would have to be someone nice.'

Donny 'We'll find them for you.'

Del 'Would you?' (*Pause.*) Although we joke about it.
(*Sighs.*) Do you want me to go and look at John?

Donny He's going to be alright.

Del Are *you* alright, though?

Donny Yes.

Del I'm sorry that I didn't find . . .

Donny (*simultaneous with 'find'*) . . . That's

Del I *looked* for him, but . . .

Donny That's al . . .

Del I Didn't find . . . I suppose I thought that – in, you
know, in addition to the things I said – that it wasn't a
good *idea* to have him come here. (*Pause.*) What business is
that of *mine*? (*Pause.*) None. None, really.

Donny That's alright.

Del Not at all. But I *looked* for him. (*Pause.*) Oh,
Donny . . .

Donny (*long pause*) Well . . .

Del Worse things have happened, I suppose. (*Pause.*) It's
such a shock.

Donny However much we . . .

Del What?

Donny I'm sorry?

Del   However much . . . ?

Donny   We could have anticipated it.

Del   How could we?

Donny   He tried to tell you.

Del   What do you mean?

Donny   He gave you the knife.

Del   I don't understand.

Donny   The Odd Gesture. (*Pause.*) Isn't it.

Del   I don't understand.

Donny   You don't understand the Gesture?

Del   No.

Donny   It was a going-away present. (*Pause.*) Going away. (*Pause.*) Big German knife. A war memento. Do you know the meaning of it?

Del   . . . meaning . . .

Donny   You know what it's for.

Del   The knife.

Donny   Yes.

Del (*pause*)   To cut things.

Donny   I mean the spec . . .

Del   The specific *purpose*? No. No. I mean *no*.

Donny   It's a *pilot*'s knife . . .

Del   . . . yes. I know that . . .

Donny   If he was forced to *parachute* . . .

Del   Yes.

Donny   He would use it to cut the *cords*. If his parachute snagged.

Del   Huh. If it snagged on what?

Donny   On a tree.

Del   Oh, you mean when he landed.

Donny   Yes.

Del   Huh. (*Pause.*)

Donny   And that's the meaning. (*Pause.*) When he was forced to abandon . . .

Del   Yes. (*Pause.*) When he was forced to *abandon* his . . . (*Pause.*) He looked for *safety*. (*Pause.*) The knife. It cut . . . It 'released' him.

Donny   Yes. That's right.

Del   . . . as *any* tool . . .

Donny   And he gave it to you.

Del   He can be very generous. Is that alright? To . . .

Donny   Yes. No. He can.

Del   He . . .

Donny   . . . what am I going to do? You tell me. Yes. He could be generous. I don't know.

Del   . . . he was opening a can. With it. And I said . . . actually, he saw me looking at the knife. And he wiped it. And gave it to me. (*Pause.*)

Donny   When you were at the Camp.

Del   That's right – (*Pause.*)

Donny   Tell me what you talked about.

Del   What we talked about in the Woods.

Donny   Yes.

Del   We talked about you.

Donny   About *me* . . . ?

Del Yes. (*Pause.*)

Donny What did he say?

Del How happy he had been.

Donny Really.

Del That's what he said.

Donny How can you understand that. (*Pause.*) How in the world . . .

Del I'm so sorry.

Donny Did you know he was leaving me?

Del No.

Donny Did you think that he was?

Del No.

Donny No? You didn't?

Del How could I?

Donny . . . he didn't . . . ?

Del No. He didn't what . . . ?

Donny Give you a sign . . . ?

Del No.

Donny How can we understand . . . how . . . *men*, you know, I'm going to *tell* you something.

Del It's funny for two grown men to go camping anyway. (*Pause.*) I don't care. (*Pause.*) Huh. I'm a *city* boy. (*Pause. He displays knife.*) And now I'm a Forester. (*Pause.*) I'm a Ranger . . . did you know there's a Fraternal Group called the Catholic Order of Foresters?

Donny Yes.

Del You knew that?

Donny Yes. Sure. (*Pause.*)

Del   I wonder what they do. (*Pause.*)

Donny   Did you say he gave that knife to you when you went camping?

Del   Yes. (*Pause.*)

Donny   When the two of you went camping. Last . . .

Del   Last week. That's right. (*Pause.*)

Donny   He gave the knife to you.

Del   Yes. He was opening a can of . . . (*Pause.*) Why? (*Pause.*) Why did you ask?

Donny   I saw it in the attic. When I went up there. To put the things away.

Del (*pause*)   What things?

Donny   When I took the camping things up. Last week. (*Pause.*) After your trip. When you came back.

Del   I don't understand.

Donny   When you came back, last week, Robert and you.

Del   . . . yes . . .

Donny   From your trip. I went up. To put the things away. And the knife was up there. (*Pause.*) It was already there.

Del   Well, maybe he went up there first, to put it back.

Donny   . . . What?

Del   I'm saying, maybe Robert went there first to put it back. When we came back. When we came back from *camping.* (*Pause.*) I'm sure that's what occurred. (*Pause.*)

Donny   You're saying that he went upstairs to put it back.

Del   Yes. Because it was precious to him.

Donny   I don't understand.

Del   It was a *war* memento. I'm saying that it was so

precious to him that he went, and *left* the stuff . . . for *you* to put away, but went upstairs and put the *knife* into the trunk himself. (*Pause.*)

Donny   Then how did *you* get it? (*Pause.*)

Del   What?

Donny   How did you get the knife?

Del   He gave it to me.

Donny   I don't understand.

Del   He gave it to me.

Donny   How could he give it to you?

Del   What?

Donny   You said he gave it to you when you were camping. (*Pause.*) How could he give it to you when you were *camping* when it was here in the trunk when you both came back? (*Pause.*)

Del   There must be two knives. (*Pause.*)

Donny   I . . . I don't understand.

Del   There must be two knives. I bet if you went in the trunk to look right now you'd see. There was another knife. (*Pause.*) Huh. What other answer could there be? (*Pause.*)

Donny   But when did Robert give the knife to you?

Del   I *thought* . . . isn't it funny? I was sure he gave the knife to me while we were camping. I guess I'm mistaken. (*Pause.*) Huh. (*Pause.*) Unless, no . . . Huh . . . I . . . I don't know. (*Pause.*) It's a mystery to me.

Donny   When did he give the knife to you?

Del   I *told* you. (*Pause.*)

Donny   He gave it to you after you . . . *wait*!

Del   What?

Donny   He came upstairs. He came up. To the attic!

Del Who?

Donny I was putting the things away. He said. Yes. 'Leave the trunk open.' (*Pause.*) He *got* it from the trunk. When you came back. He didn't *put* it there. He went up there to *get* it. (*Pause.*)

Del That could happen.

Donny What do you mean?

Del Well, that, that's not so unusual.

Donny What isn't.

Del ... for someone to do that. (*Pause.*)

Donny Did he do that?

Del It's possible. I think he did. Yes. I think *that's* ... Um. That's *exactly* what he did. I *think*.

Donny Did you go camping?

Del Yes.

Donny Did you?

Del Of course.

Donny Why did you lie to me?

Del I didn't lie. It was a slip of memory.

Donny Why did you lie to me. Del?

Del If I did I *assure* you it was, um, *you* know ...

Donny What?

Del It was ...

Donny You didn't go.

Del Who?

Donny You and Robert.

Del That's ridiculous!

Donny You never went.

Del   That's . . .

Donny   . . . Yes . . . ?

Del   Be . . . because, be . . . what are you *saying* to me? Am, am I to be *accused* of this!

Donny   Of what?

Del   Of what I *did*.

Donny   What did you do?

Del   I. Why do you say *that*? For god*sake*!

Donny   What did you do? I'll ask Robert.

Del   You can't find him!

Donny   What do you mean?

Del   He won't tell you. (*Pause.*) Alright. (*Pause.*) But: I want to *tell* you something: I knew that I should not take that knife.

Donny   Why did you take it?

Del   Be . . . because he *gave* it to me.

Donny   Why? (*Pause.*)

Del   Huh. Well, that's the *question*. (*Pause.*) *That's* what you'd like to *know*. (*Pause.*) *Isn't* it? Yes. So you could say, 'Old Del, who we thought was so loyal' . . . I know what you mean. Bel*ieve* me. (*Pause.*) Believe me.

Donny   Why did he give the knife to you?

Del   You don't want to know.

Donny   I do.

Del   *Believe* me, you don't. (*Pause.*) To shut me up. Alright? There. Are you *happy*? I told you you wouldn't be.

Donny   To shut you up about what? (*Pause.*)

Del   Because we didn't go.

Donny   What?

Del   We didn't *go*! Do I have to *shout* it for you . . . ? We stayed *home*. What do you *think*? He'd traipse off in the *wilds* . . . with me . . . ? To talk about *life*? Are you *stupid*? Are you *blind*? Who do you think you are . . . ?
He wouldn't spend a *moment* with me. Some poor geek . . . I . . . 'Robert'. 'Here's my Old Friend Del . . .' You're *nuts*, you're *stupid* if you think that's what went on. He used my *room*, alright? He said, 'Del, can I Use Your Room' Is that so weird? There. Now I've told you. Now you can sleep easier. I *told* you not to ask. Don't tell me I didn't tell you. (*Pause.*)

Donny   He used your room.

Del   That's absolutely right.

Donny   Why? (*Pause.*)

Del   To go there with a woman. (*Pause.*) And now, and now you know the truth, How weak I am. How 'Evil' I am. Because he, because he said, 'I have some things to do'. I didn't know. 'I want it to seem like I'm gone.' And so I let him in. What was I . . . huh! And you should have, *I* spent the week, slept in the, in my, my nook in the *library*. In *fishing* clothes . . . and don't you think *that* looked stupid! (*Pause.*) I . . . I, actually, I've been waiting for this. I knew that I should tell you. This is the only bad thing I have ever done to you. I'm sorry that it came out like this. But we can't always choose the . . .

Donny *starts to cry.*

Donny   Bobby . . . Bobby . . . Bobby . . .

Del   I . . . I . . . well, I'll go. I suppose. (*Pause.*) I . . .

Donny (*simultaneous with 'go'*)   Get out. (*Pause.*) Get out.

Del *exits.*

Pause.

Donny *starts to cry.*

Donny   Bobby . . . Bobby . . . Bobby . . . Bobby. Bobby.

Bobby. (*Pause.*) Bobby. (*Pause.*) Bobby. Bobby. Bobby.

John *appears in bathrobe.*

Pause.

John   Are you dead?

Donny   What?

John   Are you dead? (*Pause.*)

Donny   Why do you say that?

John (*simultaneous with 'that'*)   I heard you calling.

Donny   Go back to bed, John.

John   I heard voices . . .

Donny   . . . you should go back to bed.

John   . . . and I thought they were you. (*Pause.*)

Donny   It was me.

John   And so I said '. . . there's someone troubled'. And I walked around. Did you hear walking?

Donny   No.

John   . . . and so I went outside. I saw a candle. In the dark.

Donny   Where was this?

John   In my room. It was burning there. I said 'I'm perfectly alone.' This is what I was saying to myself: 'I'm perfectly alone.' And I think I was saying it a long time. Cause I didn't have a pen. Did that ever happen to you?

Donny   I don't know, John.

John   So I came downstairs to write it down. I know that there *are* pens up there. But I don't want to look for them.

Donny *goes to him and cradles him.*

John   Do you think that was right?

Donny Shhh.

John Do you think that I was right?

Donny Shhh.

John Mother? (*Pause.*)

Donny Shhh.

John Do you think that I was right?

Act Three

Evening. One month later.

The room is denuded. Various packing boxes are seen.

Donny I've put the kettle on.

John Thank you.

Donny I went up for your trunk.

John The movers will take it.

Donny There were some things I thought that you might like to have.

John What things?

Donny I've left them out. For the first few nights. (*Pause.*) Until the boxes come. (*She starts into the kitchen.*)

John Mother. Do you ever think things? (*Pause.*) Mother . . . ?

Donny What, do I think things?

John Yes.

Donny What things, John? (*Pause.*)

John Do you ever wish that you could die?

Donny How can I help you, John?

John Do you ever think that?

Donny . . . do I wish I could die?

John Yes. (*Pause.*)

Donny I don't know.

John Yes, you do.

Donny No, I don't know, John.

John Yes you do. You can tell me. (*Pause.*) It's not such a bad feeling. (*Pause.*) Is it?

Donny I don't know.

John Yes. You do.

Donny Things occur. In our lives. And the meaning of them . . . the *meaning* of them . . . is not clear.

John . . . the meaning of them . . .

Donny That's correct. At the time. But we assume . . . That they *have* a meaning. We . . . (*Pause.*) We *have* to because . . .

Sound of kettle whistling, off.

John I don't understand.

Donny How can I *help* you? Do you see? (*Pause.*) Do you see?

John No.

Donny At some point, do you see? At some *point* – there are things I cannot help you with. Do you see? That have *occurred*, that . . .

John I can't sleep.

Donny Well, John, it's an unsettling . . .

John . . . I want . . .

Donny . . . yes?

John I would like to go to the Cabin . . .

Donny (*simultaneous with 'Cabin'*) Well, no, John, we, we can't . . .

John That's why I can't sl . . .

Donny What do you want me to do? What, do you see? I don't know what I can do. What do you want from me? John. I am not God. I don't control the world. If you could think what I could do for you. If you could *say* it . . . But if there is nothing . . . Do you see? As if we were

simply two human beings. And I *told* this to you. As a fact.
Which . . . (*She starts for the kitchen.*)

John   I don't know what you're . . .

Donny (*off*)   John. Yes. You do. I know you're frightened.
I know that you are. At some point in our lives . . .

Kettle continues whistling, then stops.
Del *enters from front door.*

Donny (*off*)   At some point in our lives – we have to look
around, do you see? And, and take . . . we have to *accept* . . .
John: everyone has a 'story' in their lives. Did you know
that? And this is *yours*. I'm going to speak to you as an
adult. At some point . . . wait a moment . . .

Del   Hello. (*Pause.*)

John   Hello.

Del   How are you today?

Donny (*off*)   At some point in our lives, we have to face
ourselves. What kind of tea . . . ? (*Pause.*) . . . John . . . ?

Del   How are you today?

John   I'm fine.

Del   That's good.

John   What did my Mother say?

Del   I came to *talk* to you.

John (*simultaneous with 'you'*) . . . what did my mother . . .

Del (*simultaneous with 'mother'*)   She wanted to know what
kind . . .

John *gets up.*

Donny (*off*)   John . . .

Del   What sort of 'tea' you wanted. I'd like to *talk* to you
John.

John (*simultaneous with 'to'*)   I have to go upstairs.

Donny (*off*) . . . John . . . ?

John *exits*.

Donny *entering, with a tray.*

Donny Where is my son?

Del I don't know. (*Pause.*) He went upstairs. I'm sorry what I did. (*Pause.*) That's all I came to say. (*Pause.*) How are you? (*Pause.*) How is your son? (*Pause.*) 'How odd that I should be concerned.' 'After the way that I treated you.' Isn't that something? (*Pause.*) Aren't we a funny race? The things we do. (*Pause.*) And then what we say about them. You'd think, if there were a 'Deity' we would all burn. Wouldn't you . . . ? (*Pause.*) If there were order in the world. But we go on. Swine. (*Pause.*) All of us. What are we to do?

Pause.

Donny How is my husband?

Del I don't see him.

Donny No?

Del You know: I think there is a God, however. For he prompts us to do things. (*Pause.*) Wouldn't it be too terrible if our folly were our own? I wanted to come here, to 'revert' to a pagan, to a pagan, to a pagan, uh, 'mode'. (**Del** *produces a book and the knife and puts them on the table.*) And so I brought you offerings.

Donny And that's supposed to put you back in my good graces?

Del What would do that?

Donny Nothing you've brought.

Del Here is a book. It's your book, by the way. I've kept it. All these years. (*Pause.*) Perhaps that's what rotted my character. And here is the German survival knife. I was obsessed to bring it. I thought, 'Why would she want it?' But, of course, it's not for you, it's a propitiation. To the boy.

Donny   To the boy.

Del   Yes. Well. He should have it. Shouldn't he?

Donny   Should he?

Del   Yes.

Donny   Why?

Del   Because I'd wronged him.

Donny   You'd wronged him. Hadn't you wronged me?

Del   What was I going to bring you, flowers?

Donny   But you brought the boy the knife.

Del   *I* didn't deserve it. It's his Father's, um, what do they call it? 'War' memento. A 'combat' trophy ... I brought you the bb ...

Donny   ... it's not a 'combat' ...

Del   I brought you the *book* ...

Donny   It's not a combat trophy.

Del   Well, well, it's a *War* memen ...

Donny   It's not a Combat trophy.

Del   *Whatever* it is.

Donny   It's not ...

Del   Alright. He won it in the War. Why is this important to you?

Donny   He didn't win it in the war.

Del   *Really.*

Donny   No.

Del   No. The German knife?

Donny   No.

Del   Well, of *course* he did.

Donny Not in the 'fighting'.

Del Oh. He didn't . . . ?

Donny No. Not in the 'fighting'. No.

Del Well, yes, he did.

Donny How could he? He was a *flier*. Do you see?
(*Pause.*) He was a flier.

Del No. I don't see.

Donny He was a flier. What? Could he 'capture' it? In
the air? (*Pause.*) Could he get it in the air?

Del (*pause*) Then how did he obtain it?

Donny How do you think?

Del I don't know.

Donny He bought it. (*Pause.*)

Del He bought the knife.

Donny That's right.

Del Where?

Donny From a man. On the street.

Del . . . he did . . .

Donny In London.

Del Huh. (*Pause.*) You're saying he bought the knife. And
you thought that would hurt me. (*Pause.*) And you're right,
of course.

Donny . . . to hurt you.

Del Well, you knew it would.

Donny Why would that hurt you?

Del Oh, you didn't know that.

Donny No.

Del Then why did you say it?

Donny I . . .

Del That the souvenir that he gave me, as a War
Memento, was, um, with 'associations', that it had no
meaning for him. And what would I know about the war? I
live in a *Hotel*.

Donny I didn't mean to hurt you.

Del Oh, if we could speak the truth, do you see? For one
instant. Then we would be free. (*Pause. Sighs.*) I should
chuck it anyway. It's bad luck. How could it be a suitable
gift? Mmm. But I am wedded to it. As are we all. *Aren't*
we? As . . . (*Pause.*) It's a kind of bird. What is it? Um. An
Albatross? Is that the bird? The bird which I'm talking
about? 'Instead of a cross, an Albatross . . .' (*Of knife.*) It's a
piece of shit, anyway.

Donny Is it?

Del Well, if it isn't a *war* memento . . . You're damned
right. I . . . you see what it leads us to . . . ? And I don't
want to harbor, to harbor . . . 'n' I don't *want* your fucking
book. 'My blessings on this house' . . . DO you know how
long I've had it? I *hate* myself. I don't want it. Looking at it
all the time. 'Take it back', 'No, she's forgotten'. Lord. Was
ever anyone so false. Keep it. *Keep* the damned thing.

Donny *looking at book.*

Donny It's your copy.

Del It is.

Donny Yes.

Del How do you know?

Donny It's got your name in it.

Del Isn't that funny.

Donny This tea is cold.

Del It's cold, yes. (*Pause.*)

Del (*of book*) . . . this *is* my copy . . . Isn't that funny.

Because I wondered what I had done with it.

Donny My son can't sleep.

Del Oh, Lord, we live with our sins.

Donny Am I pathetic?

Del Are you pathetic? We're all pathetic. All of us. The lives we lead are trash. What we do, and what is done to us. 'Are you Pathetic' . . . *Bullshit. Bullshit.* All the fucking *dirt* we have to eat. Are you pathetic? *Listen* to me.

Donny Why should I listen to you?

Del The truest thing I know. Everything that we . . .

John *appears on the landing. Pause.*

Donny Yes, John? (*Pause.*)

John I'm cold. (*Pause.*) I'm cold. I'm sorry. My *mind* is racing. I . . .

Donny You what? (*Pause.*)

John . . . I think . . .

Donny . . . what can I do about it?

John I . . .

Donny What can I *do* about it, John?

John I don't know.

Donny What do you expec . . .

Del . . . may I speak to him?

John I don't, I'm afraid. I know that I should not *think* about certain things, but . . .

Del (*to* **Donny**) May . . . ?

John . . . but I . . .

Del John: John: I'd like to help you; Now: you have to go to sleep. You must go to sleep. If you do *not* sleep, *lay* there. Lay in bed. What you think about there is your concern. No one can help you. Do you understand? This is the most important . . . *finally, each* of us is . . .

John   Where is the blanket?

Del   I . . . *Each* of us . . .

John   . . . I want the . . .

Del   Alone.

John   . . . the *stadium* blanket.

Donny (*simultaneous with 'stadium'*)   I've put it away.

Del   . . . Each of us is alone.

John   I want it.

Donny   I've put it away, John.

John   I'm cold. Could I have it, please.

Donny   It's packed away.

John   Where?

Donny   A box. Up in the attic, I believe . . .

Del (*simultaneous with 'believe'*)   It's in the attic, John.

John   I need it. I'm cold.

Donny   *John* . . . Alright, now.

Del (*to* **Donny**)   But could he have it? Maybe he . . .

Donny   It's packed in a box.

Del   Why couldn't we get it, though, Do you see?

Donny   . . . It's . . . It's waiting for the *movers*, John.

Del   But might he have it. though?

Donny   It's wrapped up.

John   I could undo it.

Donny   Fine. Then it's in the attic. In the large brown box.

John Yes.

Donny With the new address on it.

John And I can open it. The box?

Donny If you will go to sleep. You must go to sleep. Do you hear me?

Del That is the point, do you see? John? I'm talking to you like a man.

Donny You can unwrap it. If you go to sleep. But you must *promise* . . .

John I Promise.

Donny . . . because . . .

John I understand. I promise. (*Pause.*) I promise.

Donny Do you *understand*?

John Yes. Yes. I promise. (*Exits.*)

Pause.

Del No, he . . .

Donny If I could find *one man*. In my life. Who would not betray me . . .

Del I'm sorry . . .

Donny . . . one . . .

Del I betrayed you.

Donny Everyone, all . . .

Del . . . yes.

Donny And all you do is 'give' . . .

Del . . . I know . . .

Donny . . . and . . .

Del You try to say 'human nature', but . . .

Donny I don't know what our nature is. If I *do*, then it's bad. *Men* . . .

Del   . . . I know.

Donny   If I do it's *filthy* . . . all the men I ever . . .

Del   And I'm, I'm, so sorry. To have added, one *iota*, in my stupid . . .

Donny   In this *cesspool*.

Del   *Listen* to me . . . Who am I? Some poor Queen. Lives in a Hotel. Some Silly old Soul. Who Loves you . . .

Donny   . . . who loves me . . .

Del   . . . that's right . . .

Donny   Get out. (*Pause.*)

Del   Wait?

Donny   Get out of here. Every man I . . .

Del   Oh, bullshit. You're as weak as I am.

Donny   Every man I ever . . .

Del   Well, why does it happen? (*Pause.*)

Donny   What do you mean?

Del   Is it *chance*? I *saw* it. With Robert. With *men* . . .

Donny   Get out.

Del   With the boy. You think it's some *mystery*? What we *encounter*? What.

Donny   . . . I said get out of here.

Del   What we provoke . . .

John *appears.*

Donny   And what is that? . . . *Philosophy*? . . . How *dare* you. Act as you have done. Come *in* here. *Stand* there . . .

John   I . . .

Donny   . . . you *queer* . . .

John   I ... (*Pause.*)

Donny   Yes. Yes, John, what?

John   I ...

Donny   What? What? You promised. Did you promise?

John   ... I ...

Donny   ... It's not a small *thing*. You ...

John   I only ...

Donny   Yes, *What*? *What*? 'You only ...' You prom ...

John   ... I only ...

Donny   I DON'T CARE. Do You Know What It Means To Give ... ?

John   ... I ...

Donny   ... give your *word*? I DON'T CARE.

John   ... I ...

Donny   I DON'T CARE. Just, just, just get the hell out of this room. Do you hear? I don't care. I ... I ... you *promised* me.

John   I ...

Donny   I Don't CARE. Go away. You *lied* to me. I love you, but I can't like you. You lied. I'm sorry.

John   I ...

Donny   What? You what?

Del   Here. Take the book. Go to bed. This is the book, John. I wanted you to have it. It was my copy. It's yours, now. 'My Blessings On This House'. It's yours. Off you go. If you can't sleep you read it.

John   I ...

Del   It's alright, now. You go to bed.

Pause.

John   I have to cut the twine.

Donny   . . . the twine.

John   On the box. To get the blanket. It's tied, I . . .

Donny   Go to the kitchen, take, no, they're packed. It's packed, John, you'll have to go without it.

John   You said I could have the blanket.

Donny   Well, you'll have to do without.

Del   You'll have to do without it, John. Goodnight.

Donny   Del said goodnight to you. Did you hear him? John? John?

John *starts to walk away.*

Donny   I'm . . . will you walk away when I'm speaking to you? Did you hear me? Are you blind? Can't you see that I need comfort? What must I do? That you treat me like an *animal*.

Do you want me to go Mad? Is that what you want? The man said Goodnight to you. (*Pause.*) Come here and tell the man you're sorry. (*Pause.*)

Del   It's alright.

Donny   Do you think so? (*Pause.*) No. I won't *have* it. No. You *tell* me. I'm *speaking* to you.

Del   Your Mother's waiting, John. John?

John   I hear voices.

Del   Your Mother's waiting for you.

John   . . . before I go to sleep.

Del   What does she want to hear? What does she want to hear you say?

John (*pause*)   I'm sorry.

Del   What?

John I'm sorry.

Del Alright, then. You take the knife. When you're done . . .

John I can't go to sleep.

Del . . . When you're done . . .

John I hear voices. They're calling me. Mother . . .

Donny Yes. I'm sure they are.

John They're calling to me.

Del . . . take the knife and go. (*Pause.*)

John They're calling my name.

The Old Neighborhood

**The Disappearance of the Jews
Jolly
Deeny**

The Old Neighborhood was first performed in the United States at the Hasty Pudding Theatre, Massachusetts, on 11 April 1997.

The Old Neighborhood was first performed in the United Kingdom at the Royal Court Theatre Downstairs, London, on 17 June 1998. The cast was as follows:

'The Disappearance of the Jews'

Joey	Linal Haft
Bobby	Colin Stinton

'Jolly'

Jolly	Zoe Wanamaker
Bobby	Colin Stinton
Carl	Vincent Marzello

'Deeny'

Deeny	Diana Quick
Bobby	Colin Stinton

Directed by Patrick Marber
Designed by William Dudley
Lighting by Rick Fisher
Sound by Simon Baker

The Disappearance of the Jews

Characters

Bobby, *a man in his thirties or forties*
Joey, *his friend*

Scene
A hotel room.

Joey What I remember . . . what I remember was that time we were at Ka-Ga-Wak we took Howie Greenberg outside.

Bobby Was that Howie Greenberg?

Joey Yeah . . .

Bobby No . . .

Joey No? Who was it, then?

Bobby It . . .

Joey It was Howie Greenberg.

Bobby Red hair . . .

Joey Yeah. Red hair. Braces.

Bobby That was Howie Greenberg?

Joey Yeah.

Bobby From Temple Zion?

Joey No. He never went to Zion?

Bobby No?

Joey No. Hey, Bob, no, *you* never went to Zion.

Bobby What's that mean, I don't know who went there . . . ?

Joey No. It doesn't mean that. But you know the time I'm talking of?

Bobby We tied him to the bed. We put him in the snow.

Joey Yeah.

Bobby I got to tell you something, Joey, it was not Howie Greenberg. Howie never went to Winter Camp. (*Pause.*) Am I right? (*Pause.*) Am I right? Jeff went to Winter Camp. Tell me I'm wrong. (*Pause.*) You fuckin' asshole . . .

Joey You, you, what the fuck would you know, never

even get a Christmas card from you: 'What happened to who.' It was Jeff . . . ?

Bobby   Yeah. (*Pause.*)

Joey   Isn't that funny . . . I'm not sure you're right . . . (*Pause.*) Huh . . .

Bobby   Whatever happened to Howie?

Joey   Howie.

Bobby   Yeah.

Joey   Are you ready for this . . . ? Howie turned out to be a fag.

Bobby   You're kidding.

Joey   No.

Bobby   You're kidding.

Joey   No.

Bobby   He's a fag.

Joey   That he is.

Bobby   How about that.

Joey   Isn't that something.

Bobby   Yeah. (*Pause.*) His parents?

Joey   Moved to Florida. (*Pause.*)

Bobby   I always liked him.

Joey   I did, too. (*Pause.*)

Bobby   Huh. (*Pause.*)

Joey   Yeah. (*Pause.*)

Bobby   Whatever happened to Jeff?

Joey   He's still here . . .

Pause.

I was thinking I was up on Devon . . . You 'member when
we used to take the Ravenswood . . . ?

Bobby   When? See the Cubs . . . ?

Joey   Yeah.

Bobby   Oh yeah . . . Is that joint still there?

Joey   What? Frankels . . . ?

Bobby   On Devon . . . ?

Joey   The roast beef . . . ?

Bobby   Yeah.

Joey   Yeah. It's still there. It isn't on Devon.

Bobby   No?

Joey   It's on Petersen. It's in Rogers Park. (*Pause.*)

Bobby   You 'member those two broads we had?

Joey   The Rogers Park broads?

Bobby   The folk-dancing broads . . .

Joey   . . . yeah . . .

Bobby   The two Debbies . . .

Joey   Debbie. Yeah. Right.

Bobby   Rubovitz and Rosen.

Joey   Debbie Rubovitz and Rosen.

Bobby   For five bucks, which one was mine?

Joey   I don't know.

Bobby   For ten bucks?

Joey   Rosen.

Bobby   You're full of shit.

Joey   Rosen. You owe me ten bucks.

Bobby   It wasn't Rosen.

Joey You don't know, you fuck, you're bullshitting me. You don't remember.

Bobby I remember. Mine was Rosen.

Joey That's what I said.

Bobby No.

Joey You said, 'Which one was Rosen.' I said yours.

Bobby She was? (*Pause.*)

Joey I don't remember . . .

Bobby Which was the short one . . . ?

Joey Yours. Right? With the curly hair . . . ?

Bobby And which one was her name?

Joey I don't know. (*Pause.*)

Bobby Whatever you think happened to those broads?

Joey I don't know.

Bobby You ever think about them?

Joey Very seldom. When I go through Rogers Park. (*Pause.*)

Bobby You think they were dykes?

Joey I don't know. D'you think that?

Bobby I kind of did.

Joey I kind of did, too.

Bobby At the time?

Joey No. Are you kidding me . . . ? Who knew? I tell you what I think: They were before their time.

Bobby Oh yeah . . . they were . . .

Joey They were before their time . . .

Bobby Fucking broads.

Joey I tell you how I always knew the broad was yours, the broad she couldn't find her way outta the bathroom, that was yours . . .

Bobby And what were you, a head man . . . ?

Joey Except for Deeny, of course.

Bobby . . . what. . . ?

Joey Except for Deeny. Yes, I was a head man, yeah . . .

Bobby You want to discuss, what . . . ?

Joey . . . and the broad, she couldn't find the light switch, that was yours . . .

Bobby . . . okay . . .

Joey 'Why's this black stuff coming out of the salt shaker?'

Bobby . . . some intellectual giants . . .

Joey . . . that's right . . .

Bobby 'Tell us about Moby Dick' . . .

Joey You wished . . .

Bobby And so which broad was mine?

Joey Rosen . . . I don't know . . . Rubovitz . . . Some Jew broad . . . some folk dancer. I don't know . . . some JAP . . . some Eskimo . . . (*Pause.*) How's Laurie?

Bobby Fine.

Joey Yeah, but how is she, though . . . ?

Bobby She's fine. What did I say?

Joey You said that she was fine. (*Pause.*)

Bobby All right. (*Pause.*)

Joey So? (*Pause.*)

Bobby So what?

Joey Yeah. So what, so how is she, you give me this shit all

the time . . . you never fuckin' changed you know that, Bob:
'Fuck you, I don't need anyone, fuck you' . . .

Bobby   And what are you, huh? You been reading
Redbook . . . ? What is this all of a sudden . . . (*Pause.*) You want
to know how she is? She's fine.

Joey   Well, that's all I asked. I ast you how she is, you barked
at me. Fuck you.

Bobby   Hey, you know, Joey, you know, people get
married . . .

Joey   Yeah. I know they do.

Bobby   They . . . (*Pause.*)

Joey   What? (*Pause.*) What? (*Pause.*) What? Mr Wisdom . . .
speak to me.

Bobby   I should never have married a shiksa.

Joey   Yeah. I know. 'Cause that's all that you used to say,
'Let's find some Jew broads and discuss the Talmud . . .'

Bobby   This is something different.

Joey   Is it?

Bobby   Yes. I'm talking about marriage, you asked a
question, I'm answering you. You don't want to fuckin' talk
about it, we'll talk about something that you like. (*Pause.*)

Joey   Tell me.

Bobby   You know what she said?

Joey   Who, Laurie?

Bobby   Yeah.

Joey   No, what.

Bobby   Listen to this: 'What are we going to tell the kids.'

Joey   She said that?

Bobby   Yes.

Joey   When?

Bobby   Right before I left . . .

Joey   'What are you going to tell the kids . . . ?'

Bobby   Yeah. (*Pause.*)

Joey   What *are* you going to tell the kids?

Bobby   What is there to tell? The kid is a Jew.

Joey (*pause*)   Well, Bob, the law says he's a Jew, his, you know what the law says, he's a Jew his mother is a Jew.

Bobby   Fuck the law.

Joey   Well, all I'm saying, that's what the law says . . .

Bobby   Joey, Joey, what are you saying, a kid of mine isn't going to be a Jew? What is he going to be? Look at him . . .

Joey   I'm, I'm only talking about . . .

Bobby   I know what you're talking about. What I'm saying, common sense? They start knocking heads in the schoolyard looking for Jews, you fuckin' think they aren't going to take my kid because of, uh . . .

Joey   No. No.

Bobby   Well . . . ?

Joey   What I'm saying . . .

Bobby   . . . are they going to take him, or they're going to pass him up 'cause he's so . . .

Joey   I'm talking about the law.

Bobby   'Cause he's so blond and all, 'Let's go beat up some kikes . . . Oh, not *that* kid . . .'

Joey   Hey, Bobby, don't make me out the bad guy here, I only brought it up.

Bobby   Well, listen to this, Joe, because I want to tell you what she says to me one night: 'If you've been persecuted so long, eh, you must have brought it on yourself.' (*Pause.*)

Joey   She said that?

Bobby   Yes. (*Pause.*)

Joey   Wait a second. If we've been oppressed so long we must be doing it.

Bobby (*pause*)   Yes.

Joey   She said that.

Bobby   Yes. (*Pause.*)

Joey   And what did you say to her?

Bobby   I don't know . . .

Joey   What do you mean you don't know? What did you say to her?

Bobby   Nothing. (*Pause.*)

Joey   She actually said that? (*Pause.*)

Bobby   And. (*Pause.*) And I mean it got me thinking . . .

Joey   Ho, ho, ho, ho, hold on a minute, here, ho, Bobby. Lemme tell you something. Let me tell you what she feels: She feels left out, Jim. Don't let that white shit get into your head. She feels left out. They got, what have they got, you talk about community, six droll cocksuckers at a lawn party somewhere: 'How is your boat . . . ?' Fuck that shit, fuck that shit, she's got a point in my ass, what the fuck did they ever do? They can't make a joke for chrissake. I'll tell you something, you're sitting down, the reason that the goyim hate us the whole time, in addition they were envious is; we don't descend to their level . . . (*Pause.*) because we wouldn't fight. The reason we were persecuted because we said, hey, all right, leave me alone, those Nordic types, all right, these football players, these cocksuckers in a fuckin', wrapped in hides come down and 'cause we don't fight back they go 'Who are those people . . . ?' (*Pause.*) 'Hey, let's hit them in the head.' Because we have our mind on higher things. (*Pause.*) Because we got something better to do than all day to fuckin' beat the women up and go kill things. My dad would puke to hear you talk that way. I swear to God. Alavasholem, he would weep with blood, your father, too, to hear you go that way. What are they doing to you out there? (*Pause.*) You're too shut off, Bob. You should come back here. (*Pause.*) My dad. (*Pause.*) You know, when we were growing up, he always used to say: It will happen again. We used to say, huh . . . ?

Bobby   I remember.

Joey   I used to say, 'Papa, you're here now. It's over.' He would say, 'It will happen in our lifetime.' And I used to think he was a fool. But I know he was right. (*Pause.*) I'm sorry that now he isn't here to tell him so. (*Pause.*) Because I wish he was here. (*Pause.*)

Bobby   'Vyou been out to Waldheim?

Joey   Judy and I went last month. We try to go once a month.

Bobby   Would you like to go out?

Joey   We could go. Yes.

Bobby   Just the two of us.

Joey   I know what you're saying.

Bobby   When can we go?

Joey   How long will you be in town?

Bobby   Till the weekend.

Joey   You want to go tomorrow?

Bobby   Yes.

Joey   All right. (*Pause.*) We'll go in the morning. (*Pause.*)

Bobby   I'll pick you up.

Joey   All right.

Bobby   We're really going to go.

Joey   All right.

Pause.

I'll tell you something else: I would have been a great man in Europe – I was meant to be hauling stones, or setting fence posts, something . . . Look at me: the way I'm built, and here I'm working in a fucking restaurant my whole life. No wonder I'm fat. I swear to God. You know how strong I am? We went to Judy's folks, they had a tree had fallen in the road. Up in Wisconsin . . . ?

Bobby Yeah . . . ?

Joey I picked it up. (*Pause.*) They wanted me to take a crowbar to shove it aside, the car could pass. I didn't know what they meant. Huh? I wasn't showing off . . . you know I'm strong . . .

Bobby . . . since grade school.

Joey And Arthur says, 'We got to move the tree . . .' I picked it up, I put it over there, I put it down, he's standing there, a crowbar, all their mouths are hung open. (*Pause.*) It was a big tree, too. That's what I mean, Bobby, that's where we should be, farming somewhere . . . Building things, carrying things . . . this shit is dilute, this is schveck this shit, I swear to God, the doctors, teachers, everybody, in the law, the writers all the time geschraiying, all those assholes, how they're lost . . . of course, they're lost. They should be studying Talmud . . . we should be able to come to them and to say, 'What is the truth. . . ?' And they should tell us. What the Talmud says, what this one said, what Hillel said, and I, I should be working on a forge all day. They'd say, 'There goes Reb Lewis, he's the strongest man in Lodz.' I'd nod. 'He once picked up an ox.' (*Pause.*) Or some fucking thing. I don't know if you can pick up an ox, Bob, but I tell you, I feel in my heart I was meant to work out in the winter all day. To be strong. Of course we're schlepping all the time with heart attacks, with fat, look at this goddam food I sell . . . that stuff will kill you, it killed my dad . . . it's good to harvest wheat, to forge, to toil; my father's sitting on his ass for forty years driving through Idaho for Green and Green, what did he need for nourishment . . . ? Nothin'. He should have been . . . the time should come we're sixty we look back, our wives are there, our children, the community . . . and we are sitting there, we are something . . . And we've been men. You know . . . ?

Bobby Yes.

Joey And we've lived. We've lived the life we were supposed to live. (*Pause.*) Not this, Bobby. Not this . . . (*Pause.*) I don't know. I'm getting old. I look at the snow the only thing I long that I should be in Europe.

Bobby I'm sure it was no picnic there.

Joey In Europe?

Bobby Yes.

Joey Ah, fuck, I don't know, Bob . . . I don't know . . .

Bobby Joe, with the Nazis . . . ?

Joey Fuck the Nazis. Fuck the Nazis, Bob. I'm saying, give a guy a chance to stand up . . . Give 'im something to stand for.

Bobby That's very pretty, and when they stick glass rods in your dick and break them off . . .

Joey . . . that was the Japs . . .

Bobby I'm saying, Joey, that's romantic shit . . .

Joey Is it . . . ?

Bobby Because, yes, because, yes. It is. And to a certain, yes, it is, and to a certain extent it's, I'll tell you what it's, it's profaning what they went through.

Joey Oh. Is it . . . ?

Bobby Yes.

Joey And why . . .

Bobby Because they went through it.

Joey They did . . . what I'm saying, that I could have, too, that's all I'm saying.

Bobby You don't know you could have . . .

Joey   Yes. That's what I'm saying, Bob . . . I could . . .

Bobby   . . . to go through that shit in the Camps . . . ?

Joey   Yes.

Bobby   No, Joe, no. You don't know what you would have done . . .

Joey *shrugs.*

Bobby   You don't know what the fuck you would have done, what you would have felt. None of us know.

Joey (*shrugs*)   If you say so, Bob.

Pause.

I'll tell you where I would of loved it: in the shtetl. (*Pause.*) I would of loved it there. You, too. You would of been Reb Gould. You would of told them what Rabbi Akiba said . . .

Bobby   You think they fooled around?

Joey   Who? In the shtetl?

Bobby   Yeah.

Joey   The guys in the shtetl?

Bobby   Yeah.

Joey   I think it was too small.

Bobby   But when they went to town . . .

Joey   When the guys went to town?

Bobby   Yes.

Joey   With Polish whores . . . ?

Bobby   Yeah . . .

Joey   I don't know.

Bobby   You think you would have?

Joey   No. With who?

Bobby   Or some young Jewish thing . . . ?

Joey Inside the shtetl . . . ?

Bobby Yes.

Joey And, what, defile my home . . . ?

Bobby You think you would have.

Joey You would be found out . . .

Bobby I would?

Joey Because you were a, yeah. Because you were a Jew. If you wanted to go out fuck around who'd have you? If you stayed home you would be found out. I think. (*Pause.*) But on the other hand who's to say what could go on. At night. In Europe. (*Pause.*) That's true, too . . . (*Pause.*) Judy would be old . . . she would have some incurable disease . . . we would be married years. But I would not be old. I would be deep in grief, and deep in contemplation of my life. Some young, the daughter of one of my customers, the orphaned daughter . . . is this what you're saying?

Bobby Yes.

Joey She comes to me, the whole town is silent with sympathy, 'I baked this for you.' (*Pause.*)

Bobby Righty-o. (*Pause.*)

Joey Is this what you're saying?

Bobby That's right. (*Pause.*) What did she bake?

Joey What did she bake? What did she bake? What did she bake?

Bobby (*pause*) . . . yum.

Joey (*pause*) . . . carbohydrates . . .

Pause.

Yeah, many times I wished to go back, to the war, to when my folks came here . . . to Orchard Street . . . you know, to Maxwell Street . . . to pushcarts . . . to . . .

Bobby We wouldn't have liked it.

Joey You think?

Bobby No.

Joey I don't know . . .

Bobby You know what I would, I'll tell you what I would have loved, to go, in the twenties, to be in Hollywood . . .

Joey Huh.

Bobby Jesus, I know they had a good time there. Here you got, I mean, five smart Jew boys from Russia, this whole industry . . .

Joey Who?

Bobby Who. Mayer. Warners. Fox.

Joey Fox? Fox is Jewish?

Bobby Sure.

Joey Fox is a Jewish name?

Bobby Sure.

Joey Who knew that?

Bobby Everyone.

Joey Huh. (*Pause.*) I always saw their thing, it looked goyish to me.

Bobby What thing?

Joey Their castle, that thing on their movies . . .

Bobby No.

Joey I thought it was a goyish name.

Bobby 'Fox'?

Joey Twentieth Century Fox. (*Pause.*) Century Fox. (*Pause.*) Charlie Chaplin was Jewish.

Bobby I know that, Joe.

Joey Yeah? People fool you. Oh, you know, you know who

else was Jewish? Mr White. . . .

Bobby   Mr White . . . ?

Joey   Mr White. On Jeffrey. The shoe store . . . ? Miller-White Shoes.

Bobby   . . . yeah . . . ?

Joey   On Jeffrey . . . ?

Bobby   He was Jewish?

Joey   Yeah.

Bobby   Huh.

Joey   My mom told me.

Bobby   He didn't look Jewish.

Joey   That's what I'm saying . . . (*Pause.*)

Bobby   He was a nice guy.

Joey   Yes. He was.

Bobby   I remember him. They always gave you what, a lollipop something when you came out.

Joey   Why do you think kids hate trying on shoes?

Bobby   I don't know. (*Pause.*) You know, actually I don't like trying them on either.

Joey   You don't?

Bobby   No. (*Pause.*)

Joey   I don't think that I do either. (*Pause.*) Jimmy does.

Bobby   He does?

Joey   Yeah. (*Pause.*) So I was reminiscing with my mom . . .

Bobby   . . . yeah . . .

Joey   You know, about the shoe store, huh? 'Cause I took Jimmy in to get his shoes, I'm talking about when we stopped on Pratt, I say, 'The old shoe store the goyish guy, Miller's

partner.' So she goes 'Jerry White . . .' He was the shamus,
Temple Zion thirty years.

Bobby Huh.

Joey Huh . . . ?

Bobby How about that.

Joey That's what I said.

Bobby How about that. (*Pause.*) He still alive?

Joey No. He died.

Bobby He died, huh?

Joey Yes. He did. (*Pause.*)

Bobby The store still there?

Joey Oh, Bobby, it's all gone. It's all gone there. You knew
that . . .

Pause.

Life is too short.

Bobby Life is very short.

Joey It's very short. We're sitting on the stoop, we're old . . .
(*Pause.*) We're married . . . we have kids . . . (*Pause.*)

Bobby How's Judy?

Joey (*pause*) I pray, you know, I pray every night, I pray that
I can get through life without murdering anybody.

Bobby Who would you murder?

Joey I'm saying I'm uncontrollable.

Bobby Hey, hey, you're human . . .

Joey . . . and I got married wrong. (*Pause.*) Well . . . there,
(*Pause.*) there you are.

Bobby You didn't get married wrong, Joe.

Joey Yes, I did. You don't know. I want to tell you

something, Bob, she's a wonderful woman, but there's such a thing as lust. I don't know if it's lust. Yes. Yes, it is. I, I, I say this is a feeling . . . I, I'm not alone. (*Pause.*) Then I walk out the door . . .

Bobby We all feel like that sometimes . . .

Joey You don't know what I'm going to say, I walk out of the door I say, 'If I never saw them again, it would be fine . . .'

Bobby We all feel like that sometimes . . .

Joey No, no. Listen to me. There are times, a feeling I think gets so overpowering it becomes a fact, and you don't even know you did it. Sometimes I think, 'Well if they were killed . . . if they died . . .' and sometimes I think I'll do it myself.

Bobby It's just a feeling, Joe.

Joey I pray you'll never know it. Sometimes it goes farther. I have killed them, and I take the plane, I don't call anyone, because now I don't care; and fly to Canada and rent a car and go into the forest and begin to walk . . . I know I have to die . . . so I walk . . . and I'm going north. I feel so free. I can't tell you, Bobby . . . I have a pistol, I can end it any time. I feel so free . . . If I could feel like that in my life . . . I swear there are people who can live like that. I know there are. Who exist. Holy men. Visionaries, scholars, I know they exist . . . I know they're cloistered . . . I know that it's real. But I can't get it up. I'm going to die like this. A shmuck. (*Pause.*) All of the stuff I'd like to do. I'll never do it. (*Pause.*) What do you make of that? (*Long pause.*)

Bobby You really have a gun?

Joey What gun?

Bobby You said you have a pistol . . .

Joey I said that I have a pistol . . . ?

Bobby You said you were going north . . .

Joey In my dream. In my dream . . . in my fantasy . . . you know . . .

Bobby   Oh. (*Pause.*)

Joey   In my imaginings.

Bobby   Oh. (*Pause.*)

Joey   I actually *have* a pistol. In my store.

Bobby   You do?

Joey   Behind the counter.

Bobby   Mmm.

Joey   For burglars. You worried I would shoot myself?

Bobby   You said you would.

Joey   I actually might. I think that sometimes. (*Pause.*) Don't you? (*Pause.*) Bobby . . .?

Bobby   (*pause*)   Sometimes. (*Pause.*)

Joey   I knew you did. (*Pause.*) I wouldn't take the pistol from the store, though. And I'll tell you why, because I think that just its presence, that you know it's there discourages them. (*Pause.*) Let them go rob someplace else. Everything, everything, everything . . . it's . . . I'll tell you: It's a mystery . . . (*Pause.*) Everything is a mystery, Bob . . . everything. (*Pause.*) I don't know how things work. I can hang up a coat hook, people that I know can fix a stove. (*Pause.*) Anyone can change a tire – although Lucille bought a new Pontiac, she went to change the tire, the jack wouldn't fit it.

Bobby   Maybe she wasn't putting it in right.

Joey   She said that she was. I think they gave her the wrong size, they custom things today and you can't change a fucking tire with the wrong size jack. People could die of something like that. Because everything is so far from us today. And we have no connection.

Joey   Who? Who are they? . . . and there are lives, Bobby, where people never have a thought. Where all day it is like they aren't there. Where they are a dream of their environment. Where their lives are a joy. Where questions are answered with ritual. Where life is short. We read them in the books.

Bobby   ... what books ... ?

Joey   I don't know what books ... that's what I'm saying ... but there are things ... there are things ... there ... there are ways to get there that exist. They ... (*Pause.*) In rituals, I'm saying that you didn't make up, but existed ... they would cause you pain.

Bobby   Who would?

Joey   ... they'd take you in a hut. You'd come out, you would be a man. (*Pause.*) And, by God, that is what you would be. (*Pause.*)

Bobby (*pause*)   I think I invent ceremonies, but I never keep them up. I know I should, I say if I forget this now, I'll never keep it up, but I don't.

Joey   What? Like what?

Bobby   Like anything.

Joey   Like what?

Bobby   Like prayer.

Joey   You don't keep up prayer?

Bobby   No.

Joey   What? Did you used to pray?

Bobby   I've prayed. (*Pause.*)

Joey   Judy and I joined a synagogue.

Bobby   You did?

Joey   Yeah.

Bobby   Which one?

Joey   It's new.

Bobby   Up by you?

Joey Yeah. (*Pause.*)

Bobby What do you do, you go there . . .

Joey . . . we just joined . . .

Bobby You did.

Joey Yeah. (*Pause.*)

Bobby Hey, you know?

Joey Yeah, I know.

Bobby What?

Joey I know.

Bobby (*sighs*) Joey . . . Joey . . . Joey.

Joey Bushes are steel.

Bobby Bushes are steel. What else in the world would they be?

Joey That's right.

Bobby And what's the second manhole?

Joey It's a ground rule double.

Bobby Take your base. (*Pause.*) D'you ever think that we would live to be this old?

Joey No. (*Pause.*) I never thought about it. (*Pause.*)

Bobby You think we're getting old?

Joey Yeah. (*Pause.*) I suppose we are. (*Pause.*) Isn't everybody?
Pause.

Bobby You remember the Sleepy Time Motel?

Joey Yes.

Bobby Is it still there?

Joey Yes, it is.

Bobby You remember when Joan Carpenter threw up?

Joey Yes.

Bobby Those girls. (*Pause.*)

Joey Yeah, I remember . . .

Bobby (*pause*) Joan . . . Deeny.

Joey Deeny. I see her now and then. She works at Fields.

Bobby She does?

Joey She got divorced.

Bobby I didn't even know that she was married.

Joey She got married million years ago.

Bobby When did she get divorced?

Joey Not too long, maybe a year ago. Two years.

Bobby And how is she?

Joey Yeah. She's fine.

Bobby Did she get fat?

Joey No. (*Pause.*) She's selling cosmetics on the first floor.

Bobby She is?

Joey Yeah.

Bobby She ever ask about me?

Joey Yeah.

Bobby What does she say?

Joey How were you.

Bobby What did you tell her?

Joey That you're fine. (*Pause.*)

Bobby She works at the place downtown or on Michigan?

Joey Michigan.

Bobby Cosmetics.

Joey   Yeah.

Bobby   What does she look like?

Joey   She looks the same.

Bobby   She does?

Joey   Yeah. I'm struck by that sometimes. I mean you look the same to me.

Bobby   Isn't that funny, 'cause you look the same to me.

Joey   You think that's funny?

Bobby   Yeah.

Joey   I think it's funny, too. I wish I had a cigarette.

Bobby   Yes. I do, too. (*Beat.*)

Joey   You wanna go get some?

Bobby   I almost do, but I shouldn't.

Joey   No, I shouldn't either. (*Pause.*) Isn't that something?

Bobby   Yes. It is, Joe.

Joey   Isn't that something?

Bobby   It's one for the books.

Jolly

Characters

Jolly, *a woman in her thirties or forties*
Bob, *her brother*
Carl, *her husband*

Scene
Jolly's home.

Scene One

Evening. **Jolly**, **Bob** *and* **Carl**.

Jolly ... and he said, 'I disapprove of you.' 'Of what?' I said. 'Of, well, I don't know if I want to go into it ...' 'Of something I've done ...?' I said. 'Yes.' 'To you?' 'No.' 'To *whom?*' I said. He said he would much rather not take it up. 'Well, I wish you *would* take it up,' I said, 'because it's important to me.' 'It's the way,' he said. 'It's the way that you are with your children.'

Bob (*pause*) *What?* (*Pause.*)

Jolly 'It's the way that you are with your children.'

Bob Oh, Lord ...

Jolly I ...

Bob ... how long can this go ...

Jolly I ...

Bob ... how long can this go *on?*

Jolly I wanted to, you know, I stayed on the pho –

Bob How long can this go on? *Wait a* minute. *Wait* a minute: You should call all ...

Jolly ... I know ...

Bob ... you should cease ...

Jolly ... I know.

Bob ... all *meetings, dialogue* ...

Jolly ... but the children ...

Bob You should never ... listen to me, Jolly:

Jolly I'm ...

Bob You sh –

Jolly Yes, I know.

Bob You should take an oath never to *talk* to, *meet* with . . .

Jolly . . . but the children . . .

Bob And the children most especially. How can this, are we going to expose another generation to this . . . this . . .

Jolly And the thing of it is, is . . .

Bob He said *what? What* did he say . . . ?

Jolly He . . .

Bob He didn't like the way you raise your children . . .

Jolly . . . he said that he'd been in *therapy* . . .

Bob . . . hu.

Jolly . . . and he'd, he'd come to . . . *what* was it . . . ?

Carl 'See.'

Jolly . . . he was a different *man*. From the man we knew.

Carl He'd come to 'realize' that he had 'changed'.

Jolly . . . to realize that he had changed, yes, and the things which, in a prior life, he might have 'suppressed' . . .

Bob . . . that's their way. That's their way. That's their swinish, selfish, *goddam* them. What *treachery* have they not done, in the name of . . .

Jolly . . . I know . . .

Bob . . . of 'honesty'. God *damn* them. And always 'telling' us we . . .

Jolly . . . yes.

Bob . . . we were the bad ones . . .

Jolly Well, we were.

Bob . . . *we* were the bad ones.

Jolly And when he said it, I heard his father's voice.

Bob   Well, *fuck* him . . .

Jolly   And I saw. He'd turned into his father.

Bob   . . . he didn't like the way you raise your kids . . .

Jolly   And so, you know, I knew, I *remembered*. Way back. They were . . .

Bob   . . . they were sweet kids.

Jolly   *He* was a sweet kid.

Bob   . . . she . . . ?

Jolly   *He* was a sweet kid, Buub. You weren't there . . .

Bob   I was there for part of it.

Jolly   NO. You weren't there, you know. You weren't there. *I* was there. I see where it all comes from. Both of them, the traits . . .

Bob   . . . Yes.

Jolly   . . . and they had . . . I don't mean to excuse them. I don't want to *excuse* them.

Bob   . . . there's no excuse for them.

Jolly   No. I believe that. And I am not a vindictive person.

Bob   No.

Jolly   I'm not, Buub. I've been thinking of this . . .

Bob   I know that you're not.

Jolly   And I think about all those years . . .

Bob   They treated you like filth. (*Pause.*)

Jolly   Yes. They did. They treated me like filth. Do you know, you don't know, 'cause you weren't there – when they first came. *Mother* told me, I was ten. So she was, what eight; she was going to sleep in my bed. She took up the bed, as she was a 'creeper', you know. I'm a rock. You put me in a bed. And unmoving. Morning. She was all over the place. And I went in and told Mom that I couldn't sleep. She said, 'She is his daughter, and this is the case. If you can't sleep, sleep on the floor.'

Bob   No.

Jolly   . . . and . . . yes. And she wouldn't let me take the covers. (*Pause.*)

Carl   . . . and she wanted to call him back.

Bob   Call him back.

Carl   Yes.

Bob   And say *what?*

Jolly   I was so . . . *astonished*. By the phone call . . .

Bob   Someone calls me up, says, 'I don't like the way you raise your kids . . .'

Jolly   I was, you know, like sometimes when you are in *shock* . . . ?

Bob   . . . yes.

Jolly   The most bizarre events seem 'commonplace'.

Bob   . . . yes.

Jolly   I was . . . because you know, I called HIM. He didn't call *me*, I called him. *This was the thing of it:* The kids. My kids. They were *close* to him. When he and Susan first got married . . .

Bob   . . . yes . . .

Jolly   They used to, they'd say: 'What do your kids like to do? What are a list of their favorite . . .'

Carl   . . . activities.

Jolly   . . . and we would write them *down* . . . and they would come over and take the kids, and take the *list* and do all of them.

Bob   Hm.

Jolly Do *all* of them. Five things in a day and they'd do *all* of 'em . . . and *loved* the kids. So. Since we've moved. And we had not *heard* from them. For six months. So I picked up the phone . . .

Bob . . . that was your mistake.

Jolly I picked up the phone. And I called them. 'How are you? Sorry we haven't . . . "called" you' . . . and the stress of *moving* . . . 'pause.' Is there something *wrong*? Is something the *matter*? No. He doesn't want to talk about it. 'What is it?' and then . . .

Bob And then you have to wrench it from him . . . 'Please *tell* me . . .'

Jolly The 'counseling'. He's '*changed*'. . . . He's come to see.

Bob . . . uh huh . . .

Jolly How he was re –

Bob He was repressing his feelings.

Jolly Yes. He was repressing his –

Bob About the way you raise your kids . . . ?

Jolly Well, you know, and the *counseling,* and *she* is in the counseling and all this psychobabble. And they never took 'responsibility' for any aspect of the things, you know, the things that they were 'feeling'. . . . It's all . . . 'I.' 'Me.' 'What I feel.' Oh, oh, he said he's learning – you're going to love this: He's learning to live 'facing his past'.

Bob Facing his past.

Jolly Facing his past.

Bob Well, of course. Of course. That's how they *all* live. Facing the past. Facing the past. Looking at the past. *Fuck* him. AND fuck 'counseling', is the thing I'm saying . . .

Jolly . . . I'm with you.

Bob Fucking leeches.

Jolly 'Counseling.'

Bob Hey? Y'don't need a *roofing* counselor. You need, you
may need a *roofer*, tell you 'get a new roof'. You don't
need, *sit* there, five years, five hours a week, *talking* about
'Do we need a roof. Do we need a roof.' (*Pause.*)

Carl Tell him. (*Pause.*)

Jolly You know, he told me, when he did Mom's
estate . . . ?

Bob Her estate? She never had a thing of her own, her
whole life.

Jolly Hold on. I went to him, you know, all her
antiques . . . ?

Bob He's selling them. I know.

Jolly He *sold* them.

Bob . . . he sold them?

Jolly He *sold* them. He kept saying, 'Anything you want,
just *tell* me . . .'

Bob . . . he sold them . . . ?

Carl Yes.

Jolly So I *told* him. Everything I said . . .

Bob . . . oh, no.

Jolly You know, and anything I'd ask for . . .

Bob . . . yes.

Jolly He'd say, 'Waaaaalll . . . that's a very special *piece*
. . . uh. Huh huh.' What do I get? NOTHING.
NOTHING. Nothing. Some cheap . . . and it doesn't *matter.*
(*Pause.*) But she was my mother. And I was there while she
was dying. *I* was there. *I* was there. He'd drop her off, and
I was left, an infirm woman. Fourteen hours a day. And
when she'd wake up at night, and my two kids, and no
'Nurse', no. And he could afford it . . . *I* couldn't . . .

Bob   . . . no . . .

Jolly   *He* could. And just drop her off. And sonofabitch that *cunt* that *cunt* that *Carol*. DIDN'T EVEN COME TO THE . . .

Bob   . . . I know . . .

Jolly   . . . the *funeral*. And who gets the armoire?

Bob   Which?

Jolly   In the hallway. And who gets the mink coat? (*Pause.*)

Bob   . . . I know . . .

Jolly   Couldn't spare the time . . .

Bob   . . . yes . . .

Jolly   . . . from her *counselors* . . . who are, what, going to teach her how to Lead a Good Life . . . ? Fuck HER. And all the married *men* she's screwing. As her way. Of expressing herself, and could not even come to Mom's *funeral*. And he says, 'What do you want, Jolly . . . ?' And I *tell* him.

Bob   . . . yes . . .

Jolly   Nothing very valuable, God forbid, except that it had a meaning for me. AND EVERY PIECE, Buuby, that I say . . .

Bob   . . . I know . . .

Jolly   He tells me *why I cannot have it*. Until . . .

Bob   . . . of course . . .

Jolly   I stop asking.

Bob   . . . I know . . .

Jolly   . . . because . . .

Bob   . . . I know, Jol . . .

Jolly   . . . because, because . . . (*Pause.*) So . . . so . . . he sold them. (*Pause.*)

Carl   Tell him about the money.

Jolly   I don't care about the money.

Carl   Tell him.

Jolly (*sighs*)   So he says. So he says . . .

Carl   He's 'sold' the stuff . . .

Jolly   So he says the proceeds are in an 'estate'.

Carl   A trust.

Bob   A trust, I know.

Jolly   So he says . . . *I* say, you know, we are having some tight times, we could really *use* some of the money . . .

Bob   . . . uh huh . . .

Jolly   'It's in a trust.' Uh huh. Round and round. Then he says, 'I could, you know, perhaps I could *invade* the trust . . .'

Bob   . . . invade the trust . . .

Jolly   Yes. 'If it's . . . if it's truly . . .'

Bob   . . . why did it have to be 'truly'. . . ?

Jolly   Wait. It gets worse. (*Sighs.*) So. Round and round. I call. You know. This and that. The *kids*. 'I really could *use* the money. We are really – you know . . . "*moving*" . . .'

Bob   . . . yes.

Jolly   . . . when we thought we were moving . . .

Bob   I know.

Jolly   'And we're really *tight* now . . .' (*Pause.*) 'And we could use some help.'

Bob   . . . I know what it cost. To ask him.

Jolly   For 'ten thousand dollars' . . . (*Pause.*) the way he lives. 'Ten thousand dollars' . . . Long long pause. 'Waal . . .' I jump in. Whatever it took, that it took, out of the 'will', I don't mean the will, what do I mean, the . . . ?

Carl . . . estate.

Jolly The 'estate'. 'Whatever it took, out of the estate. From . . .'

Bob . . . God damn him.

Jolly . . . from Bill and Carol . . .

Bob (*softly*) God damn him . . .

Jolly 'Whatever it took, just, if I have to *sign* something, I'll sign whatever . . .'

Bob . . . yes.

Jolly '. . . and subtract . . .'

Bob . . . of course . . .

Jolly 'And just give me my "portion" *now*. (*Pause.*) And we really *need* it.' (*Pause.*) Because we did.

Bob . . . I know you did.

Jolly And he says 'no'. (*Pause.*) Just 'no'. (*Pause.*) Just 'no'.

Carl She asked him to invade the trust and he said, 'No.' (*Pause.*)

Jolly . . . Oh. Oh. And it gets better. He didn't say, 'No.' He said . . . he said, 'I am not convinced I would invade the trust if I *could*.' (*Pause.*)

Bob What does that mean?

Jolly Well, *that's* what it means. (*Pause.*) Are you hungry, Carl?

Carl A little.

Jolly Mmm. I'll get it in a minute.

Carl All right.

Pause. **Jolly** *sighs.*

Bob How are you doing, Carl?

Carl   I'm fine.

Bob   Holding on?

Carl   Oh, yeah. I'm holding on. (*Pause.*) How about you Bob? (*Pause.*)

Bob   You ever get tired of this? You must. It's the same. Isn't it? Every year.

Carl   . . . it's the same . . .

Bob   . . . our family.

Carl   Yes. It's the same.

Bob   Don't you get tired of it?

Carl   Well, I tell you . . . (*Pause.*)

Bob   Yes . . . ?

Carl   It's what it is, Bob.

Jolly   And they made fun of us.

Bob   They . . .

Jolly   You know they did. Carl and me. '*Jolly* . . .'

Bob   Uh huh . . .

Jolly   'I'm sure that he's a fine "man", Carl . . .'

Bob   Uh huh . . .

Jolly   'But "we want to say" . . .'

Bob (*to self*)   'We want to say . . .'

Jolly   'Your mother and I want to say . . .'

Bob   Well, that was how they were . . .

Jolly   *Wasn't* it . . .

Bob   Yes.

Jolly   *Wasn't* it?

Bob   Yes.

Jolly   And . . . the shit at Christmas. You know, you know, Marshall Fields . . . ? She would take me to Fields. 'What do you think?' Some dress. If I *wanted* the dress, I would have to say 'naaaaah'. She would take me back. 'I think it rather suits you.' 'No, uh . . . it's . . . it's "pretty", Mom, *but* . . .' And of course, she would *buy* it for me. But if I said, 'God, what a gorgeous dress.' Hey. You know what? Hey, you know what I'm going to *tell* you something: 'fuck her, *though* she's dead.' (*Pause.*) Fuck *her*, and fuck the *lot* of 'em.

Bob   . . . they never loved us.

Jolly   They, no, Buub, in their 'way' . . .

Bob   Jol, Jol, that's, that's your *problem* . . .

Jolly   What is? What is?

Bob   I say that I'm gonna sue the cocksucker. You say no. I mean. What in the hell *possesses* a man. To *treat* you like that: Do you see: It's *cruel*, Jol. *They're cruel*. They were *cruel* toward us, and if there's such a thing as 'abuse', we got it. And *your* problem is . . .

Jolly   I know what my problem is . . .

Bob   . . . your problem . . .

Jolly   I know what my problem is . . .

Bob   *Your* problem is: You could not face the fact. They didn't love you. And that's your problem. That they did not love us. (*Pause.*)

Jolly   They loved *you*, Buub.

Scene Two

Middle of the night. **Bob** *and* **Jolly**.

Jolly   'If you don't want it . . .'

Bob   'No, no, no, I *like* it.'

Jolly   'Waal, if you *don't* like it, you can take it back.'

Bob   'I like it.'

Jolly   'Waal. If you *don't*. If you find . . .'

Bob   'No, I *like* it. I *do*. I think that it's . . .'

Jolly   'Waal, your mother and I, only want to *say* . . .'

Bob   'I think that it's . . .'

Jolly   'You take it back. We "saved the slip" . . . and . . .'

Bob   . . . fucking *right* I'm going to take it back. Because what would I *do* with it?

Jolly   You remember the skis?

Bob   The skis.

Jolly   I remember the skis. I wanted the skis. (*Pause.*) I wanted skis that year.

Bob   You don't ski, Jol.

Jolly   *Why* don't I ski? Bobby? (*Pause.*) Oh shit. (*Sighs.*) I just, you know, the thing of it, the thing of it is, I just wanted some skis. Would it have killed them to've given me a pair of skis? Was that so ludicrous? A monster like myself? Was that so . . . (*Pause.*)

Bob (*softly*)   . . . yes . . .

Jolly   Christmas Day. (*Pause.*) Christmas Day.

Bob   I know.

Jolly   She . . .

Bob Wait, wait, I remember.

Jolly You . . . ?

Bob I remember . . .

Jolly You remember what?

Bob Christmas Day. A plaid . . . a . . . a plaid something.

Jolly A . . .

Bob . . . that they gave me.

Jolly . . . yes?

Bob A plaid . . .

Jolly A reversible raincoat.

Bob That's right.

Jolly A reversible raincoat.

Bob . . . what did I do?

Jolly Monday morning. Took it back to Fields.

Bob I took it back to Fields.

Jolly And traded it in.

Bob That's right.

Jolly For what?

Bob I . . . ? What? No, I've forgotten. Oh, my God. Jol. For what, then, a year . . . ?

Jolly . . . easily . . . easily . . .

Bob For a *year*. 'Where is that raincoat, Bubby . . . ?

Jolly '. . . we gave you for Christmas. That you liked so much?'

Bob 'I left it at the . . .' Ah. Ah. Wait. Wait. Jol. Wait, wait, wait. I went back to Fields.

Jolly Um hmm.

Bob   TO SEE COULD I BUY BACK THAT COAT.

Jolly   That's right.

Bob   . . . could I buy back the raincoat.

Jolly   That's right, Buuby.

Bob   Could I buy back the Fucking Raincoat to stop the questions as to where was the raincoat. That I was so grateful for.

Jolly   . . . that's right.

Bob   That stupid raincoat. And that woman at Fields. Sent to fucking *Germany* to see, could they replace that raincoat.

Jolly   That's right, Bobby.

Bob   And calling her back. And calling her back Thursday, and oh, what a pathetic fucking thing. (*Pause.*) My plaid. My Plaid Reversible Raincoat. (*Pause.*)

Jolly   And, you know, I'm thinking, all of this, 'If you don't *like* it, you can take it back . . .' If they had *loved* us. Mightn't they have *known* what we might want? I know what *my* kids want. (*Pause.*) I know what *my* kids want. It's not that difficult. It's Just Not. I'm sorry. Carl says . . . Carl, say what you will. I'm sorry, every weekend, Every weekend. You know what we *did* last weekend? They had friends sleep over. We made *popcorn*. We made *fudge*. Next morning we made *pancakes*. You know, you know, I turned into a fine cook.

Bob   I know you did.

Jolly   No, I mean, you ain't seen *nothing* here . . .

Bob   It was fantastic . . .

Jolly   I mean a *fine* cook.

Bob   Jol, I had the dinner . . .

Jolly   That was nothing.

Bob No. It was fantastic.

Jolly No, I mean, Carl, you know, I wanted to do it, for him . . .

Bob . . . uh huh . . .

Jolly Because before *Carl* you know . . .

Bob Uh huh . . .

Jolly Before *Carl* . . . I . . .

Bob I remember, Quiche Soup . . .

Jolly . . . I couldn't Drop an Egg.

Bob Uh huh . . .

Jolly Why *should* I . . . ? Hummm? *She* never taught me . . . She never taught me a *thing* . . . I'm in here, the girls. *Every night* . . . Every Night I'm in here . . .

Bob I saw them.

Jolly And they're learning to cook.

Bob I know.

Jolly You see, Bob? Do you see? This is a *family*. (*Pause.*) *And some day*, Bob. I'm going to be dead. Some day, *they* are going, they are going to be in a kitchen. And they're going to say. To their girls . . . '*My* mom . . .' (*Pause.*) Because this is a Family. You see? 'My mom used to do it this way.' (*Pause.*) 'This is what my mom taught me.' (*Pause.*) And every weekend. We had a four-hour session of, we played *Monopoly*. We, God forgive us, we went *bowling*, we . . .

Bob . . . the kids seem so . . .

Jolly . . . we rented a *film* we thought they and their friends would enjoy. And Carl, God bless that man, do you hear?

Bob Yes.

Jolly God *bless* him. And they'd say: 'Jol: *Jolly*. We, waaal, he just . . .' And 'We don't feel . . .'

Bob   Uh huh . . .

Jolly   'Your mother and I. "Just Don't Feel" that *Carl* is the Right Sort.'

Bob   Mmm.

Jolly   The Right Sort. The right fucking sort. Huh? For who? For a piece of shit like me. For a piece of shit they *despised*. Like me.

Bob   . . . mmm . . .

Jolly   Am I wrong? For us. And what in the world gave them that right? Who never thought a *moment* of my happiness . . . ? Eh? And the *finest* and the *best man*, and he *loved* me, you understand? That was the thing, do you see, that disqualified him, Bob. He loved me. That was what they hated, Bob. For how could a man who loved *me* be any good? BUT WHOSE MARRIAGE WORKED – (*Pause.*) WHOSE MARRIAGE WORKED? Out of the *pack* of them. Three generations. And I don't mean you, Buub . . .

Bob   No, I . . .

Jolly   No, I don't mean you. I mean of them. Who Had the Marriage That Worked? And it's been, what has it been, 'easy'?

Bob   No.

Jolly   You are Fucking in Hell *Right* it hasn't. And, you know. When we thought we would have to move. Out of *work*. And she'd come, 'Mom' . . . She'd come to see us . . . 'Mom' . . . (*Pause.*)

Bob   It's okay, Jol. (*Pause.*) It's okay. (*Pause.*) It's okay, Jol.

Jolly   Gimme a cigarette.

Pause. He gives her one.

I can't smoke these.

Bob   Break the filter.

Jolly I can't smoke these.

Bob Yes, you can. (*She smokes.*)

Jolly When we were moving. We Had No Cash, Buub.

Bob I know. (*Pause.*)

Jolly And she would come. (*Pause.*) And I'd say, 'Mom
. . . you know . . .' she'd first, she'd say, 'What do the kids
need?' And I'd say 'Shoes. They need shoes.' (*Pause.*) Well,
you know how kids . . .

Bob I know . . .

Jolly . . . grow out of shoes.

Bob I know.

Jolly *You* know what they cost . . .

Bob Yes.

Jolly Uh huh. 'The Kids Need Shoes.' The end of her
stay, she would give them, God bless her, these, two,
incredibly expensive, what are they, 'vanity' sets. A desk. A
desk to put on makeup . . . a 'vanity set'?

Bob . . . I don't know . . .

Jolly And I would say . . . *Carl* would say 'forget about
it'. I . . . I'd say . . . No. 'Mom . . . Mom . . .' (*Pause.*)
'Mom . . .' And the fucking *skis*. The *Christmas* skis. One
thousand generations we've been Jews. My mother marries
a sheigetz and we're celebrating Christmas.

Bob . . . hey.

Jolly . . . huh?

Bob Mockeys with a Mistletoe . . .

Jolly Isn't it . . .

Bob Yes. It is. (*Pause.*)

Jolly Jingle Bells. (*Pause.*) Ah, what the hell. (*Pause.*) And
The Big Present. (*Pause.*)

Bob   I remember.

Jolly   I'm sure that you do.

Bob   The Big Present.

Jolly   'Waal, we've opened *everything* . . .'

Bob   'Oh, *wait* a second . . . "What Is That Behind the Door." '

Jolly   And the fucking skis year it was this expensive, this, Red Leather Briefcase. And I was behaving badly. I was behaving oh so badly. And the one time in my life I said 'no'. And I said 'no'. God *knows* where I got the courage. I said *no*. And I was 'behaving hysterically'. I got sent to my room. And 'why must I ruin these occasions?'

Bob   Why did you ruin those occasions, Jol?

Jolly   Well, that's right. I *ruined* them . . . I *ruined* them . . . because I was an Ungrateful Child. Why did *you* ruin them, Buub?

Bob   Because I was an ungrateful child.

Jolly   I know that you were. (*Pause.*) You know, and I *carried*, I had to *carry* that fucking red briefcase for three or four years, all day, every day, full of books, These Are Your Skis. Did I tell you . . .

Bob   What?

Jolly   I had a dream about her.

Bob   About Mom . . .

Jolly   Uh huh. (*Pause.*) I'll tell you later. Can I tell you later. You know, because, what was I saying? (*Pause.*) Hm . . .

Bob   The Red Briefcase.

Jolly   Yes. (*Pause.*) You know, the girls. So adore having you here.

Bob   It's good to be here.

Jolly   You . . . it's good of you to come.

Bob   Jol . . .

Jolly   No, I know that . . .

Bob   Jol, I've been, well *fuck* 'remiss' . . . It's been criminal of me not to . . .

Jolly   I know. You've got a Busy Life . . .

Bob   No, I've just . . .

Jolly   Buub . . .

Bob   Hey, I've been *lazy*. I'm sorry. I *owe it* to you. I've been . . .

Jolly   . . . and I know it's been a difficult time for you, Buub . . . (*Pause.*)

Bob   And so I came here to get Comfort.

Jolly   Times of stress, you . . .

Bob   Isn't that 'selfish' of me . . . ?

Jolly   . . . times of stress, you . . . We need comfort. You think that you can do without it? You can't. (*Pause.*) You can't, Bob. (*Pause.*) No one . . . (*Pause.*) Carl and I . . . you know, many times . . . (*Pause.*)

Bob   How are you getting on?

Jolly   We're . . . (*Pause.*) Hey, what the fuck are you going to expect. From the Sort of a Background That We Come From. It's a miracle that we can Wind our Watch. (*Pause.*) That's what Carl said about you. And, you know . . . how *good* you're doing.

Bob   He said . . .

Jolly   He said that he knows. How incredibly *difficult* this has been for you, and he thinks that you are doing, that he thinks that you are doing well. And *that's* the man, you understand . . . that's the man they made *fun* of. That they said 'wasn't good enough for me'. (*Pause.*) *Fuck* them. Fuck the *lot* of them. (*Pause.*) And carried that fucking *bookbag* around for three years. (*Pause.*) What are you gonna do?

Bob   About?

Jolly   About your life. (*Pause.*)

Bob   I don't know.

Jolly   You don't know. Tell me. You gonna go back to her?

Bob   I don't know.

Jolly   'Cause I wanted to tell you. If you *do*. No one's going to think you foolish. I swear to you.

Bob   I'm not going back to her.

Jolly   If you *do*. (*Pause.*) I'm not saying you *should* . . .

Bob   I un . . .

Jolly   Or you should *not*. But if you *do*, always . . .

Bob   . . . I know . . .

Jolly   You remember, Bob. Carl, Carl said it: He said it, baby. You, you can *Kill the Pope*, and you are wel . . .

Bob   I'm not going to go back . . .

Jolly   . . . if you *should*. And I am not 'plumping' for it.

Bob   I know. (*Pause.*)

Jolly   I WANT ONE THING. And that is: The thing that is best for you. Period. Paragraph. And the rest of the world can go to hell. I don't give a fuck. I'm too old. (*Pause.*) And there you have it and that's the story of it. (*Pause.*) All I want to say . . . (*Long pause.*) . . . Fella comes up to me, I'm driving, fella comes up to me I'm drivin' the girls somewhere, 'Don't you know,' No. 'Did you know. This is a One-way Street . . .' I'm . . . never in my life, Bob. I'm sick. I'm a sick woman. I know that. I'm aware of that, how could I not be. My mind is racing 'Did you know,' 'Didn't you know . . .' Did I drive down on

PURPOSE? I did *not* know ... IS YOUR QUESTION ...
what? The proper, I would say, response, is 'One-way
Street!' Smiles. One way. You, we would *assume*, did not
know that you are, why *would* I, and even, I HAD, how
terrible is that. Some piece of shit JUST LIKE ME. Whether
or *not* I knew, your ... your 'rights' end with 'this is a one-
way street,' and what I MAY HAVE KNOWN is none of
your *concern*, and FUCK YOU, and I'm SEETHING at
this, this emasculated piece of shit who has to take out his
aggression on some haggard, sexless, unattractive *housewife*,
with her *kids* in her station wagon ... (*Pause.*) and this is
my fantasy life. (*Pause.*) A rich, 'full' life. (*Pause.*)

Bob   You should go to bed.

Jolly   Why should I go to bed?

Bob   Because you have a husband up there. (*Pause.*)

Jolly   I thought you gave up smoking.

Bob   You know, sometimes I can't ... I can't, it seems I
can't ... (*Pause.*) Oh, God, I get so *sad* sometimes, Jol. I
can't, it seems, getting up from the *table* ... (*Pause.*) I wake
up in the night. 'Where am I?' Three times in a night.
And I saw that I was waking up.

Jolly   To go pee the kids.

Bob   To pee the kids. You get a Red apple.

Jolly   Your kids are going to be okay.

Bob   No, they won't. Of *course* they won't. *We're* not
okay ...

Scene Three

Morning. **Carl**. **Bob** *comes in.*

Carl   How did you sleep?

Bob   Like a rock or like a baby. (*Pause.*)

Carl (*to* **Bob**)   You know, he *dumped* this stuff here.

Bob   Jolly was telling me. (*Pause.*) What was it?

Carl   It was *trash*, you'd say. It was . . .

Bob   . . . *my* stuff . . .

Carl   Your stuff. Stuff you couldn't want. Canceled *checks*. Twenty years old. It was nothing anyone could ever want to keep. Just some . . . 'trash', really . . . (*Pause.*) You know. There was so much stuff Jolly wanted. Some of your mother's . . . When he sold the house. (*Pause.*)

Bob   How can you put up with it?

Carl   Well what 'it', then . . . ?

Bob   The misfortune of our family. Do I overstate the case . . . ?

Carl   Oh, I don't . . . that's a very personal question, isn't it?

Bob   Yes. It is.

Carl (*pause*)   Well, you know. I love Jolly.

Bob   . . . are we that . . . are we that . . .

Carl   That what?

Bob   Are we . . . you know, I feel so *pathetic* sometimes, Carl.

Carl   Well . . .

Bob   No, what can you say about it?

Jolly *enters.*

Jolly   Sleep well?

Bob   Yes.

Jolly   How well?

Bob   Very well.

Jolly   Why?

Bob   'Cause I feel 'safe' here.

Jolly   How safe?

Bob   Very safe.

Jolly   Safer than Other Places . . . ?

Bob   Yes.

Jolly   Safer than Anyplace Else in the World?

Bob   Yes.

Jolly   Well, hell then.

Bob   Hey.

Jolly   That's what I'm telling you. (*Pause.*) The girls say goodbye.

Bob   Goodbye to *them*. (*Pause.*)

Jolly   Um. Call me when you get where you're going.

Bob   Why?

Jolly   So I'll know you got there. (*Pause.*) You okay?

Bob   Yeah.

Jolly   Thanks for coming.

Bob   Oh, hell.

Jolly   No, no. Thank you. We . . .

Carl   Jol, he wanted to come.

Jolly   Was I talking to you . . . ?

Carl   No. Goodbye, Bob.

Bob   Goodbye, Carl.

Jolly   Did you know, this stupid shmuck. Drove two hours to Hillcrest to pick up three boxes of, turned out to be, drafts of your *term* papers, something, junior high. (*Pause.*) Carl . . . ?

Carl   Bye, Hon.

Jolly   . . . canceled *checks*. Something. Cocksucker: He calls up: 'We have some stuff of Bob's . . .' Carl drives there to pick it up. Like fools. We, he goes over there. It's garbage. That they saved. We're s'posed to take it. (*Sighs.*)

Carl   Bye, Hon.

Jolly   See you at six.

Carl   Yes.

Jolly   The girls at gymnastics.

Carl   Yes, I know. Bye, Buub.

Bob   I'll see you, Carl.

Carl   You hang on.

Bob   All right.

Carl   Thank you for coming.

Bob   It was good to come.

Jolly   He was glad to come. He was glad to come. One time in nnnnnnn years, you *should* be glad to come. A house full of folks who love you.

Carl   Goodbye, Bob. (*To* **Jolly**.) Bye, Sweetheart. (*He exits.*)

Jolly   Don't go. (*Pause.*) We could go back. To Seventy-first Street is where we could go. To the Jeffrey Theatre. And Saturday kiddie shows. Twenty-five cartoons and a western. For a quarter. And the Chocolate Phosphate at J. Leslie Rosenblum's, 'Every Inch a Drugstore.' Do you remember? Dad, he used to take us there?

Bob   Yes. I do.

Jolly   Do you remember how it smelled?

Bob   Yes.

Jolly   And we'd go to the Peter Pan Restaurant. On the corner of Jeffrey, and get a Francheezie, and the French fries, and a cherry Coke. And we would go to the South Shore Country Club, where they wouldn't let us in. And we would sit in the window in the den, and Dad would come home every night, and we would light the candles on Friday, and we would do all those things, and all those things would be true and that's how we would grow up. And the old men, who said that they remembered Nana. Back in Poland. And, oh. Fuck it. Oh the hell with it.

Bob   I never came to see you.

Jolly   *I don't care* . . .

Bob   . . . I never came . . .

Jolly   No. I don't care . . . (*Pause.*) Oh, Bobby. (*Pause.*) Oh, God . . . And I'm having this dream. How's *this* for dreams . . . ? They're knocking on my door. All of them. 'Let me in,' and I know that they want to kill me. *Mother: Mother's* voice, from just beyond the door: 'Julia, Let Me In.' 'I will not let them hurt you . . .' the sweetest voice. 'You are my *child* . . .' and it goes on. 'I won't let them hurt you, darling . . . you are my *child*. You are my *child*. Open the door. Oh. *Julia.* I will not let them Hurt You. OH. My Dear . . .' I open the door, this sweetest voice, and there is *Mom*, with this *expression* on her face . . . (*Pause.*) And she wants to kill me. (*Pause.*)

Bob   Well.

Jolly   . . . and I knew that she did. So why did I open the door . . . ? (*Pause.*) Isn't that the thing of it.

Bob   'Thank God it was only a dream . . .'

Jolly   Yes. (*Pause.*) Isn't that a mercy . . . ? (**Carl** *re-enters.*
Pause. Picks up sheet of paper.) The address of the gymnastics.

Carl   Mm.

Jolly   What a good man.

Carl   What are you doing?

Jolly   We're being bad. We've been bad. We're being
punished. And we're going to go to our rooms. And cannot
come out until we're prepared to make, a . . . what is
it . . . ?

Bob   A Complete and Contrite . . .

Jolly   A Complete and Contrite Apology. (*Pause.*)

Carl   Do you want me to stay home?

Jolly   No. Thank you. Bobby will be here a while, you
see. And he's the only one who knows. (*Pause.*) 'Cause he
was *there* . . .

Deeny

Characters

Deeny
Bobby Gould

Scene
A restaurant.

Deeny (*pause*)　They say there's going to be a frost tonight.

Bob　Do they?

Deeny　Yes.

Bob　Y'always liked that.

Deeny　Yes. I did. It made me wish I had a garden. (*Pause.*)

Bob　Uh hmm.

Deeny　You know?

Bob　Yes.

Deeny　And you could go out to it, the morning; and see, well, you could go out to it the night before, and 'cover' things ... cover things, or 'bring them in'. (*Pause.*) You could, certain spots, they put smudge – is that the word? Smudge pots, you know, not a very pretty word, is it?

Bob　No.

Deeny　To keep the plants warm. (*Pause.*) But I was saying, in the morning. You would go out, do you know, even, well, I was going to say To Get Up Early, but I think that if you were a gardener you probably *would* be up early. Do you think?

Bob　Yes.

Deeny　... out of *love*. (*Pause.*) Rather than what? Rather than ... what?

Bob　Rather than a sense of duty.

Deeny　Yes.

Bob　... or the two would be one.

Deeny　Well, that is the thing I'm *saying*. *Isn't* it?

Bob　I know.

Deeny That would be love.

Bob Indeed it would.

Deeny And I had a vision of *coffee*. Coffee, certainly ... I *thought*, you see, I *thought* that the unfortunate thing about it was that it closed us off. And that *coffee* ...

Bob ... yes.

Deeny *Coffee*, or *cigarettes* tended to ...

Bob ... to ...

Deeny ... *paralyze*.

Bob Yes.

Deeny ... natural functions, you see, in that the one, with the digestion, or the other, with the lungs, cut down our ...

Bob ... our ...

Deeny ... abilities ... to ... to ... (*Pause.*) you know, to *use* the world, I think – those things of the world we could take in: food, or air, you know, and *use* them. Perhaps. So we say, 'It's too much.' I had a vision of a frosty morning. Myself with a cigarette. And with a cup of coffee. Smoking. As I look out of my window. And I see a garden. In this garden there are plants that I have planted and perhaps I have raised them from seeds or cuttings, do you know? The way they do ... ?

Bob Tell me.

Deeny To raise them inside, you know, from the year before. They call it 'forcing'. Or they call something else forcing, and they call this something else. (*Pause.*) But that's a nice word, isn't it?

Bob What?

Deeny Forcing.

Bob Forcing. Yes.

Deeny   If you think about it. As, you know, as 'bringing out'. These little green cups. Seeds that you have put in by the radiator. In the most ... (*Pause.*) Wait a moment. (*Pause.*) In the most safe and in the most protected of all settings in the world. *Otherwise,* they would not be born, (*Pause.*) you see; and that is what I saw when I looked out the window. (*Pause.*) I think about sex sometimes, and I think about all the times you think of a thing and vary between thinking that 'it is a mystery', and 'it is a convenience'. And many times, you do not know which of the two it is. Do you think of that?

Bob   I think that of various things.

Deeny   Of what?

Bob   Of life, of work. Of sex, of success.

Deeny   Of *all* things.

Bob   I think.

Deeny   You go back and forth.

Bob   Yes.

Deeny   Without a certainty.

Bob   Or with one which changes.

Deeny   ... and I think about the stupid *molecules.* Whatever the smallest unit is. They always tell us, in the newspapers, every day, some new unit, and you think, 'surely *this* is, the thing you tell us now, must be the smallest unit.' Or, 'you should,' you think, 'you should confess that there *is* no end to it. That there *is* no smallest unit, and it is your *science* that is lacking,' do you know? '. . . either the *instruments* or the humility to say, "There is no end to it." ' And oriental faiths, you know, posit a *pathway,* or say there is an extra *nerve* in the spine, science cannot find, the 'third eye', they're talking about. Or, or an 'aura', and I think: 'Yes, well, of course, you can approach it through *spiritual* practice,' you know, what, what, I suppose that you would call it 'faith'; it isn't that much different from believing something we see in the newspaper.

Bob   Faith.

Deeny   Not much, really. Or believing some, some
spiritual thing. It's just something that someone says is true.
And you say, 'Yes. I'll believe that that's true.' (*Pause.*) But
having lost the feeling that things will right themselves.
(*Pause.*) What? It becomes harder. Because I never, more
importantly, nor, will I. I never *planted* a garden, nor *will* I
plant a garden, and when I *question* myself as to *why*, I have
no answer.
'Would it give you pleasure?'
'Yes.'
'Would you enjoy it?'
'Yes.'
'Would it be difficult to do?'
'No.'
'Then why do you not *do* it?'
And there is no answer, but, do you know, do you know
what I mean, but it is . . . waiting . . . that's a funny word
. . . it's waiting, waiting, just beyond . . . you know, it's in
the back of my mind. 'It's because . . .' What? What is it
because? It's too much *trouble?* No. No, you see, I say to
myself, that it's the *opposite* of trouble. It's *joy*. Well, then, I
say. Well, then, draw yourself up and *do* it. And I say
'perhaps I will'. Perhaps I will.

Bob   . . . that things will not come right . . .

Deeny   Well, they *won't, will* they . . . ? (*Pause.*) In the
world. The, the, the, world . . . and I was talking about
'faith'. And you say 'this is ending'. Well, then, there's
another thing. And that will take its place. And sometimes
that's okay. But then, sometimes, that's just cold comfort.
Isn't it?

Bob   Yes.

Deeny   How d'you think I'm going at my job?

Bob   I think you're doing fine.

Deeny Yes. I do, too. I enjoy it so much.

Bob I can see that you do.

Deeny And, do you know, as you grow older – all the things you said, 'They must be true, because they're "platitudes".' Or, what is it, what is it they say? That's not what they say. What do they say?

Bob It's a cliché because it's true.

Deeny 'It got to be a cliché, because it was true.' But if you think about it, if that's its reward, that's a poor reward. Isn't it? It was *true* . . . what it used to be was *true*, and did it so well that it *got* to be the *other* thing, which is that we ignore it, but what was I saying?

Bob That it is true, *although* we have heard it so often that we tend to discount it. That to do something truly well you have to love it.

Deeny . . . and they think so at work, too, because they're going to offer me, oh, you don't want to hear it, you may want to hear it, I don't want to tell it; how could it, do you know, how could it *interest* you? Because it's like you're walking through a part of town, and you say, 'You see that house? I used to live there.' 'Really.' What can it *mean* to them? Nothing. It means something to *you*, you see, as it should. (*Pause.*) But the other person, they feel lonely. Or I wanted to say, 'It's not much, but it's *mine*.' (*Pause.*)

Bob I know.

Deeny I know you know. (*Pause.*) 'It's not much' . . . eh? 'But it's . . .' And what *could* it mean to you? You know? As the phrase is 'anyway', because it truly couldn't. It's nothing. It's . . . a bit of *buying. Ordering,* mainly, accountancy . . . 'Accountancy'? 'Accounting' . . . Bookkeeping . . . I keep track of some things. There really is a bit of buying. Everyone thinks that they've got good taste. Everyone thinks 'Everyone thinks that they've got good taste, but I *have* got good taste . . .' (*Pause.*) But I *have* got good taste. And I like it, and they like me, and there you have it. What a success story. How's *your* life?

Bob As you see. (*Pause.*)

Deeny I was thinking of tribes that *mutilate* themselves, and it occurred to me, that, perhaps, when they *do* it, they ... (*Pause.*) they get *pleasure* from it. Those tribes that ... tattoo their faces, or they stretch their lips, you know, or *necks*, or the terrible things they do to their sexual, sexual equipment; but I thought, if you know that this is terrible, as you do, and know you are frightened, which is to say, you *are* frightened, and you know that *it is the community* that forces you, then might you not feel, might you not feel, as they *did* it, you see ...: 'Yes. Yes. I surrender.' And you *die*. You undergo the pain of, the pain of, the pain of giving birth to yourself. And that *sorrow* of *years*...

Bob ... yes I understand.

Deeny ... that sorrow of years. Is condensed, do you see, into a *ceremony*. And then it is over. (*Long pause.*) Looking at the 'old thing'. Looking at *regret*. What is it we hope to gain by looking at it? Do we think it *raises* us ...? No. Do you know, it's not important.

Bob What is important? (*Pause.*)

Deeny What is important? (*Pause.*) You know, couldn't you say of *anything* that it is folly? Except passion. While you're feeling it, and afterward, *especially* of that. That it is folly. (*Pause.*) That everything is folly.

Bob Yes. You could say that.

Deeny People with sorrow in their eyes ...

Bob ... yes ...

Deeny ... you know ... people you wouldn't be *drawn* to when you were young.

Bob No.

Deeny You wouldn't see them.

Bob No.

Deeny   But they would see *you*. Maybe they'd be *attracted* to you. (*Pause.*) Some older person. Looking down.

Bob   Yes, looking down.

Deeny   But could not *have* them.

Bob   Who could not?

Deeny   The older person.

Bob   Have what?

Deeny   Have that younger love.

Bob   Have *passion* . . .

Deeny   No.

Bob   Because . . . ?

Deeny   Well, *you* know why then, *don't* you. Because it had passed. Well. And the *things* we did. And things we said. To other lovers. And the *jokes*, the private jokes, you know, and *poignancies;* and all the revenge we foreswore, *and that we could not have*. Always, and *turning*, don't we? Toward death – Do you think? Do you think so? (*Pause.*) And, you know, and the things we'd given up. When you elect it's consolation to grow up. And it *is* consolation. *But So What?* And the things we kept *till we grew sick of them*. The treasured pivots of our *world* – until . . . (*Pause.*)

Bob   'Until one day . . .'

Deeny   *Oh* yes. (*Pause.*) I never knew what you wanted. (*Pause.*) I thought I knew. (*Pause.*) I thought that I knew. (*Pause.*) *Finally* . . . (*Pause.*) And I said. (*Pause.*) They say there's going to be a frost.

Bob   Well, then, I am sure that there is.

Deeny   I am sure that there is, too. (*Pause.*) *Despite* the fact that they say it.

Bob   That's my girl.

Deeny   And it will grow cold. You know, and you used to

say, 'How Jolly.' I'm sure you still say it; though to other
people, of course, and I don't blame you. For why should
we change? Do you know? If there were something I could
do for you, I'd do it. (*Pause.*) Or for myself. Even to
proclaim, you know, that this world is a shit hole. If I just
could find it true. (*Pause.*) Did you come to say goodbye?
(*Pause.*)

Bob   Yes.

Deeny   Goodbye, then.

Bob   Goodbye. (*Pause.*)

Deeny   Goodbye, then, love. (*Pause.*)

Bob   Goodbye, love.

Methuen Contemporary Dramatists
include

Peter Barnes (three volumes)
Sebastian Barry
Dermot Bolger
Edward Bond (six volumes)
Howard Brenton
  (two volumes)
Richard Cameron
Jim Cartwright
Caryl Churchill (two volumes)
Sarah Daniels (two volumes)
Nick Darke
David Edgar (three volumes)
Ben Elton
Dario Fo (two volumes)
Michael Frayn (three volumes)
John Godber (two volumes)
Paul Godfrey
John Guare
Peter Handke
Jonathan Harvey
Declan Hughes
Terry Johnson (two volumes)
Sarah Kane
Bernard-Marie Koltès
David Lan
Bryony Lavery
Deborah Levy
Doug Lucie

David Mamet (three volumes)
Martin McDonagh
Duncan McLean
Anthony Minghella
  (two volumes)
Tom Murphy (four volumes)
Phyllis Nagy
Anthony Nielsen
Philip Osment
Louise Page
Stewart Parker (two volumes)
Joe Penhall
Stephen Poliakoff
  (three volumes)
Christina Reid
Philip Ridley
Willy Russell
Ntozake Shange
Sam Shepard (two volumes)
Wole Soyinka (two volumes)
David Storey (three volumes)
Sue Townsend
Michel Vinaver (two volumes)
Arnold Wesker (two volumes)
Michael Wilcox
David Wood (two volumes)
Victoria Wood

Methuen Modern Plays
include work by

Jean Anouilh
John Arden
Margaretta D'Arcy
Peter Barnes
Sebastian Barry
Brendan Behan
Dermot Bolger
Edward Bond
Bertolt Brecht
Howard Brenton
Anthony Burgess
Simon Burke
Jim Cartwright
Caryl Churchill
Noël Coward
Lucinda Coxon
Sarah Daniels
Nick Darke
Nick Dear
Shelagh Delaney
David Edgar
David Eldridge
Dario Fo
Michael Frayn
John Godber
Paul Godfrey
David Greig
John Guare
Peter Handke
David Harrower
Jonathan Harvey
Iain Heggie
Declan Hughes
Terry Johnson
Sarah Kane
Charlotte Keatley
Barrie Keeffe
Howard Korder

Robert Lepage
Stephen Lowe
Doug Lucie
Martin McDonagh
John McGrath
Terrence McNally
David Mamet
Patrick Marber
Arthur Miller
Mtwa, Ngema & Simon
Tom Murphy
Phyllis Nagy
Peter Nichols
Joseph O'Connor
Joe Orton
Louise Page
Joe Penhall
Luigi Pirandello
Stephen Poliakoff
Franca Rame
Mark Ravenhill
Philip Ridley
Reginald Rose
David Rudkin
Willy Russell
Jean-Paul Sartre
Sam Shepard
Wole Soyinka
Shelagh Stephenson
C. P. Taylor
Theatre de Complicite
Theatre Workshop
Sue Townsend
Judy Upton
Timberlake Wertenbaker
Roy Williams
Victoria Wood

Methuen World Classics
include

Jean Anouilh (two volumes)
John Arden (two volumes)
Arden & D'Arcy
Brendan Behan
Aphra Behn
Bertolt Brecht (seven volumes)
Büchner
Bulgakov
Calderón
Čapek
Anton Chekhov
Noël Coward (eight volumes)
Eduardo De Filippo
Max Frisch
John Galsworthy
Gogol
Gorky
Harley Granville Barker
    (two volumes)
Henrik Ibsen (six volumes)
Lorca (three volumes)

Marivaux
Mustapha Matura
David Mercer (two volumes)
Arthur Miller (five volumes)
Molière
Musset
Peter Nichols (two volumes)
Clifford Odets
Joe Orton
A. W. Pinero
Luigi Pirandello
Terence Rattigan
    (two volumes)
W. Somerset Maugham
    (two volumes)
August Strindberg
    (three volumes)
J. M. Synge
Ramón del Valle-Inclán
Frank Wedekind
Oscar Wilde

Methuen Classical Greek Dramatists

Aeschylus Plays: One
(Persians, Seven Against Thebes, Suppliants,
Prometheus Bound)

Aeschylus Plays: Two
(Oresteia: Agamemnon, Libation-Bearers, Eumenides)

Aristophanes Plays: One
(Acharnians, Knights, Peace, Lysistrata)

Aristophanes Plays: Two
(Wasps, Clouds, Birds, Festival Time, Frogs)

Aristophanes & Menander: New Comedy
(Women in Power, Wealth, The Malcontent,
The Woman from Samos)

Euripides Plays: One
(Medea, The Phoenician Women, Bacchae)

Euripides Plays: Two
(Hecuba, The Women of Troy, Iphigeneia at Aulis,
Cyclops)

Euripides Plays: Three
(Alkestis, Helen, Ion)

Euripides Plays: Four
(Elektra, Orestes, Iphigeneia in Tauris)

Euripides Plays: Five
(Andromache, Herakles' Children, Herakles)

Euripides Plays: Six
(Hippolytos, Suppliants, Rhesos)

Sophocles Plays: One
(Oedipus the King, Oedipus at Colonus, Antigone)

Sophocles Plays: Two
(Ajax, Women of Trachis, Electra, Philoctetes)

Methuen Student Editions

METHUEN DRAMA
MONOLOGUE & SCENE BOOKS

☐ CONTEMPORARY SCENES FOR ACTORS (MEN)	Earley and Keil	£8.99
☐ CONTEMPORARY SCENES FOR ACTORS (WOMEN)	Earley and Keil	£8.99
☐ THE CLASSICAL MONOLOGUE (MEN)	Earley and Keil	£7.99
☐ THE CLASSICAL MONOLOGUE (WOMEN)	Earley and Keil	£7.99
☐ THE CONTEMPORARY MONOLOGUE (MEN)	Earley and Keil	£7.99
☐ THE CONTEMPORARY MONOLOGUE (WOMEN)	Earley and Keil	£7.99
☐ THE MODERN MONOLOGUE (MEN)	Earley and Keil	£7.99
☐ THE MODERN MONOLOGUE (WOMEN)	Earley and Keil	£7.99
☐ THE METHUEN AUDITION BOOK FOR MEN	Annika Bluhm	£6.99
☐ THE METHUEN AUDITION BOOK FOR WOMEN	Annika Bluhm	£6.99
☐ THE METHUEN AUDITION BOOK FOR YOUNG ACTORS	Anne Harvey	£6.99
☐ THE METHUEN BOOK OF DUOLOGUES FOR YOUNG ACTORS	Anne Harvey	£6.99

• All Methuen Drama books are available through mail order or from your local bookshop.

Please send cheque/eurocheque/postal order (sterling only) Access, Visa, Mastercard, Diners Card, Switch or Amex.

☐☐☐☐☐☐☐☐☐☐☐☐☐☐☐☐

Expiry Date:_____ Signature: _____

Please allow 75 pence per book for post and packing U.K.
Overseas customers please allow £1.00 per copy for post and packing.

ALL ORDERS TO:

Methuen Books, Books by Post, TBS Limited, The Book Service, Colchester Road, Frating Green, Colchester, Essex CO7 7DW.

NAME: _____

ADDRESS: _____

_____

_____

Please allow 28 days for delivery. Please tick box if you do not
wish to receive any additional information ☐

Prices and availability subject to change without notice.

For a Complete Catalogue of Methuen Drama titles
write to:

Methuen Drama
215 Vauxhall Bridge Road
London SW1V 1EJ

or you can visit our website at:

www.methuen.co.uk